To my late father, Hubert Ellis (1916-1996), who bought me a typewriter when I started secondary school, and Beverley Hamilton, who did not allow us to forget our history.

ACKNOWLEDGEMENTS

I would like to thank Jackie Lewis, Ama Gueye, Reanne Ellis, Elisha Brown, Elaine Bailey, Enomwoyi Damali, Barbara McCauley, Cherry Potts, Arthur Torrington, Alan Cross, Kash Ali, Jamar, Terry Wheeler and Arif Ali for their comments and suggestions as well as their encouragement that enabled me to complete this book.

Illustrations: Lasmin Ellis
Photographs: Barbara Ellis

A Brief, but moſt True

RELATION

Of the late Barbarous and Bloody

PLOT

Of the *Negro's* in the Iſland of

BARBADO'S

On *Friday* the 21. of *October*, 1692.

To Kill the Governour and all the Planters, and to deſtroy the Government there Eſtabliſhed, and to ſet up a New Governour and Government of their own.

21. Jan. 169⅔

In a *LETTER* to a Friend.

S I R,

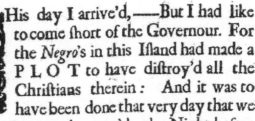
His day I arrive'd,——But I had like to come ſhort of the Governour. For the *Negro's* in this Iſland had made a P L O T to have diſtroy'd all the Chriſtians therein: And it was to have been done that very day that we came hither. But as it happen'd, the Night before it was found out very providentially, by Two of them that were a talking of this their wicked Deſign; who being fully overheard to diſcourſe thereof, they were taken up, and Examined, and ſo
frankly

frankly confeffed (when it could not be help'd)
what their Defign was. Upon which difcovery,
the Government hath taken up between two and
three hundred *Negro*'s : And Tryed and Condemn-
ed many of them. Of which Number of the Con-
demn'd perfons, Many were Hang'd, and a great
many Burn'd. And, (for a Terror to others,)
there are now feven Hanging in Chains, alive, and
fo Starving to Death. It is reported, they defign'd
to have taken up the Sirnames and Offices of the
Principal Planters and men in the Ifland, to have
Enflaved all the Black men and Women to them, and
to have taken the White Women for their Wives.
This PLOT was formed by the *Negro*'s that were
born in the Ifland, and no imported *Negro* was to
have been Admitted to partake of the Freedom
they intended to gain, till he had been made Free
by them, who fhould have been their Mafters. The
old Women (both Black and White) were to have
been their Cooks, and Servants, in other Capacities.
And they had chofen a Governour among themfelves, and every thing was prepared and fetled
in Readinefs for giving the Fatal Stroak. They
have been contriving of this Wicked and Bloody
defign this three years, and had fo long kept it very
fecret until the very day before it was to have
been done. But we hope in a little time to fee a
Stop fully put to their Contrivance, and the Vil-
lains themfelves fpeedily difcovered and detected.
Adieu.

January 18th. This may be Printed *Edmund Bohun.*

"In a letter to a friend", London, 1693 Image reference N.W 0031, as shown on
www.slaveimages.org. In Jerome S. Handler's *Slave Revolts and Conspiracies in
17th Century Barbados*, New West Indian Guide Vol 56 (1982), pp-5-43, sponsored
by the Virginia Foundation for the Humanities and the University of Virginia Library.
Courtesy of authors Jerome S. Handler and Michael L. Tuite Jr.

CONTENTS

PART TWO

FOREWORD

"Slavery is theft, theft of a life, theft of work, theft of any property or produce, theft even of the children a slave might have."
Kevin Bales in A. Stuart's, *Sugar in the Blood* (2013) p.18

Every gathering, conspiracy, insurrection or uprising on the islands and the mainland of South America were attempts, first by the Taino and then the African peoples to regain their freedom. They wanted and intended to use their labour to benefit themselves, their families, their community and their respective motherland.

Violently and callously, the planters and their government brutally suppressed their efforts to retake their freedom. The Christmas Rebellion of 1831-32, was a direct demand to the planters by the Africans; to be paid for the work they were ordered to do, in what they knew was their Christmas holiday. The young Baptist lay preacher Deacon Sharpe, instructed his congregation not to work during their Christmas break unless they were paid. The slave masters had laughed at and scorned their request to be paid for this work, so the enslaved Africans set their plantations on fire.

In response to their rebellion, the British government passed the Act of Abolition in 1833. The Act would come into effect, in August 1834. As the 1st of August 1834 approached, the planters and the British government informed the enslaved field Africans, that they would have to work a further six years without pay. Incensed by the British Parliaments' deception, many Africans

11

took advantage of the clause inserted in the 1833 Act, as it gave them the right to buy their freedom. Industriously, they farmed their small plots of land in their own time and sold their surplus crops. They used the money, to buy their freedom from the slave masters. At the same time, the planters received compensation from 1835 onwards, to free their remaining slaves after the six years were up.

In 1938, a hundred years after they had emancipated themselves, the Africans from across the Islands and the South American mainland, demanded that the lands of the sugar plantations be turned over to them. They believed that they had been promised to them, as compensation for their more than three hundred years of free back breaking labour, in the planters' cane pieces.

The current coalition of the first peoples of the islands and the Americas, as well as the African Diasporas' demand for reparation, is part of a historic campaign for social and economic justice for these peoples. Relentlessly, the African Diaspora have called for compensation from the countries of Portugal, Spain, The United Kingdom, France, The Netherlands, Denmark and Sweden without positive results. However, they will continue to do so until their demands are fully met.

'An African Journey' part one and two, presents the Diaspora's experience and perspective. This gives parents, teachers, social and youth workers the opportunity to work with children and young people, from both the Diaspora and Europe. Together, they can learn and reflect on their entangled economic and social history, as part of their personal and social development programmes. It also gives them the chance to, discuss and debate the demands by the Diaspora for economic and historical justice, for the past labour of their ancestors, that is to say, reparation.

First and foremost, the history curriculum of all the colonising nations – Great Britain, Spain, Portugal, France, The Netherlands, Denmark and Sweden – should ensure that the intertwined histories and economies of the world's peoples are taught in all schools. The history of these European nations demonstrates without a doubt that there are no 'stand-alone economies, histories or peoples in Europe, past and present'. This approach to the teaching of their interrelated history will empower pupils and the youth, to make informed decisions about their interwoven past, as well as the urgent need for economic and social justice now.

Finally, the curriculum of the islands and the South American mainland should lay emphasis on the resistance and resourcefulness of their students' ancestors. It should highlight their pupils' and students' responsibility, now, to build on the legacy of their illustrious ancestors. This will help to bring about more just and equitable societies through an understanding of their interconnected economic and world history. BEE

INTRODUCTION

It is a universal truth that the Africans, who were brutally ensnared and stolen from their compounds and villages, forcefully resisted their enslavement. Likewise, those who had enslaved them were equally determined to wring from these stolen peoples, every ounce of their labour. They intended to build an empire, to accumulate and consolidate their wealth, power and influence in their homelands; as well as in their newly acquired colonies, on the islands and the mainland of the Americas.

Thus, the battle began between the most powerful nations in Europe at the time; and the almost powerless and weaponless Taino and African peoples. Ferociously, this battle raged on the mountaintop precipices, in the swampy interior of the South American mainland; until the Africans liberated themselves, from the planters and their governments' brutality and greed.

The planters on the islands and the mainland of South America had set up a money-making enterprise, to get the maximum from growing tobacco, coffee and later the very high-priced commodity sugarcane. This created untold wealth for them. They drafted laws to justify their vicious use of the enslaved peoples. Plantation slavery based on force and brutality was designed to control and crush, the natural resistance of the Taino, African and other Amerindian peoples, to their enslavement as beasts of burden.

The planters and their government revived old laws and created new ones. These laws described the enslaved Taino and African peoples as, 'lazy, uncivilised, infantile, treacherous and devilish heathens', who threatened their life, security and wealth in their newly acquired colonies. The plantation system needed compliant labour, that would just grow the sugarcane it demanded.

Naturally, the Taino and African peoples resisted their enslavement. If the planters used their legal systems, the whip and brutal punishments to control them; they too developed successful systems to withhold their labour from them. They jumped from sailing vessels into the sea, they forced the galleons transporting them onto the shoreline and freed themselves. They poisoned themselves and the planters to end plantation slavery. The women aborted the foetuses of the planters and those sent to impregnate them so that their children would not labour in the cane pieces. They fled to the mountaintops of the islands and the South American mainland. They waged continuous and victorious war against the planters and the British army, thus forcing them to pass the Act of Abolition in 1833.

An African Journey tells the story of the rebellious Taino and African peoples. These populations fought the greed, materialism, arrogance and racism of the planters and their governments thus ending plantation slavery. They also tell the story of the continued resistance of their descendants. These communities were and are forced daily to confront oppression, exploitation, discrimination and racism in every region of the Western World in which they live.

Unbelievably, in the 20th Century Britain, the descendants of the Africans who liberated themselves from slavery have had to fight unrelenting battles against the racism, ingrained within the fabric of British and other Western societies. Their continued struggles in Britain against racism brought about some 'equality legislation'. These very limited equality concessions gave them access and some rights in a few areas of the workplace and in the education sector. The 1976 Race Relations Act and its 2000 amendment, attempted to outlaw racial discrimination in all areas of British society.

Astonishingly, as the 21st Century progressed, these invited workers witnessed successive British governments and many institutions undermine the very limited 'equality legislation and practices' which they had wrung from the society. The covert and overt practices of successive administrations and organisations have had dire consequences for the educational and financial advancement they had struggled for and achieved; these must once again be fought for.

The hidden, as well as the overt practices of consecutive governments and institutions, would inevitably return the majority of these workers and their children to the lowest level of British society. They would be part of the mass of low-paid or unskilled labour in the society, and as such would continue to be exploited by the commercial and business enterprises of the descendants of the planters. Descendants who were reasserting their financial power and economic dominance at the expense of the white working class and African-Caribbean workers from the end of the 1980s.

In the 21st Century, white skins still continue to confer excessive levels of privileges and economic power. However, people with black and non-white skins continue to face a social

Africans fleeing from their potential enslavers. Source: Coelho. P (1981) Akapwitchi Akaporo, Armas e Escravos. Instituto Nacional Do Livro e do Disco. Maputo, Mozambique.

and economic system which exploits their labour mercilessly for profit. Hourly, they live with the institutionalised and now brutal and acceptable face of racism within British and many other Western societies. BEE

Stolen from Africa. Source Coelho. P (1981) Akapwitchi Akaporo, Armas e Escravos. Instituto Nacional Do Livro e do Disco. Maputo, Mozambique.

Africans escape the Atlantic crossing. Source: Coelho. P (1981) Akapwitchi Akaporo, Armas e Escravos. Instituto Nacional Do Livro e do Disco. Maputo, Mozambique.

Part One

CHAPTER 1

Hard times

"Cattle were taken from distant compounds, and they are now amongst us," declared Chief Mkhululi gravely.

"When crops fail when animals die, and our communities want for food and water, our traditional ways of living are tested. Recently, in these gatherings we have had to deal with the unacceptable actions that have crept into our compounds and our larger community. Everyone of us here today must be vigilant, we must stand firmly against these acts and unacceptable conduct at all times," stated Elder Cabral.

"Our traditions and culture teach us that honesty and concern for others must guide us at all times. If we stray from these principles, we will bring shame and ruin on ourselves in the future. The cattle must be returned before dawn," instructed Elder Sankara quietly but firmly.

The seated elders peer far into the distance; they hoped to catch a glimpse of the future yet to come. At the same time, crops, animals as well as the inhabitants of the compounds, wilt under the blazing sun scorching Africa's soil. The elders' ceremonial robes marked the importance of the moment.

The cooling shade of the Nyala tree faded, as the elders tottered into the heat and glare of the blazing sun. The verdict of the elder council would begin a chain of actions, which they could not imagine, in their combined years on the African soil.

Moving across the grasslands, the cattle moved with the rhythm of a shadowy figure, back to their compound to joyous owners and the defeat of the thief.

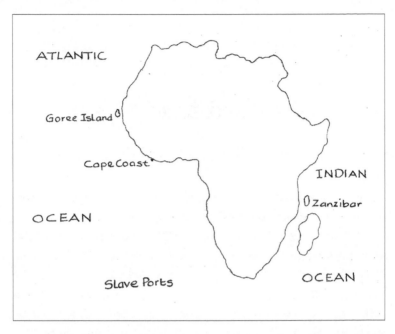

An outline drawing of Africa and Madagascar. Zanzibar, Goree Island and Cape Coast were some of the slave ports.

"I'll return a rich man one day and show them," the thief muttered uncertainly.

The gravity of the elders' meeting gave way to the eager carefree cries of children. They acted out the stories, they had heard so many times under extensively shading trees. Nightly, these stories had carried them off into soothing sleep, in their compounds.

"I want to be Anancy, and you can be Brother Lion," screeched Kesi.

"You're always Anancy, it's not fair, I want to be Anancy today," whined Ade, almost toppling over.

"Ok," snapped Kesi, "tomorrow you can be Anancy, and I will be Brother Lion."

"I'm coming to get you Anancy," roared Brother Lion fiercely.

"Come on then," beamed Kesi in delight.

CHAPTER 2

A companion

I am Anancy the storyteller, a man and spider from the African continent. Firstly, I will show how the enslaved Africans from across mainland Africa, survived the horrors of the trek to the coastal forts, the galleons and the plantations. Secondly, I will also show how they carried in their souls, the treasures of Africa and left them along the way. Then finally, how they ended slavery with their defiance, strength, intelligence as well as their courage, in their enforced home away from their motherland.

Suddenly, my body ached and throbbed, as sharp instruments sunk into my flesh while thick netting enclosed my body. Blood gushed from my wounds. Instinctively, I turned into my spider shape to escape from my cruel captors, unlike my brothers and sisters trapped in their ensnaring nets.

Quickly, I climbed into the nearest tree, I spun a steely web. Dazed and bleeding, I saw the comings and goings of the human thieves. I heard the terrifying screams of children, women and men. I saw their fear and pain, as they were thrust through the thick terrain. Inwardly, I wept as men, women and children in tatters, bound and shackled were driven and beaten by their club-wielding captors.

My wounds ached and stung. I cursed my obnoxious brothers for their betrayal, brutality and heartlessness towards their own. Fast and furiously, my throbbing limbs plucked the young gourds from my shelter and pelted them. They fled in panic to a nearby clump of bushes, to hide and work out who was attacking them.

Swiftly, the stronger captives seized the opportunity. They hauled themselves with their clinking chains, into the dense

Anancy praises his ancestors and comforts his traumatised brothers and sisters.

undergrowth and to freedom. Eagerly, the ailing captives roused themselves to follow, but their shackled feet and maimed limbs stopped them, as they shuffled hastily to escape. The despicable thieves emerged from their dump, to recapture their most valuable and agile Africans. However, a barrage of fruit bombarded them for the second time. They withdrew to their stinking hole and cursed their invisible foe.

At sunset, under the cover of darkness, the wretched creatures crawled from their slimy hole on their bellies. They rounded up their dwindling band of captives. They forced them along narrow clearings, towards the horrors of the coastal forts; they did not know was waiting for them. As they were driven, their punctured bodies began to decay. Their stagnant blood caked and matted hid their perforated skin, which little by little drained away their spirit and life. Daily, hourly, they left behind their pain and suffering, as they dragged the remaining life left in their bodies, towards the coast. As they fell or gave up on their horrific journey, the wild animals and vultures circled and feasted on, their fresh and rotting flesh.

On this journey, there would be fewer Africans chained and huddled together, in the forts and makeshift places around the

West and East African coasts. Forts and temporary places, on Goree Island off the shoreline of Senegal, Elmina Fort and Cape Coast Castle on Ghana's coastline or Zanzibar Island off the coast of East Africa. At these coastal stopovers, the frail and dejected survivors were thrown into makeshift shacks, to be fattened and revived for the impending journey. Oils and herbs were rubbed into their skins, to heal their decaying wounds. Every day pounded plantains, yams, maize and boiled vegetable leaves were stuffed into their mouths, to strengthen them for sale and shipment. Before long, they would be sold for a few colourful trinkets, trifling sums of money or some Cowry shells. The sturdy and physically fit survivors were thrown into rough and ready holding stations along the coast, to await a full human cargo before being shipped.

If my brothers and sisters had suffered unimaginable terrors and death on the trek to the coast, the second stage of their journey would be beyond human imagination. Their fate would be decided by the trade winds, the greed and temperament of the slave traders and their own resilience, while crammed into the microscopic bowels of sailing galleons. Imprisoned in their floating tombs; their bodies inevitably erupted into festering and bleeding wounds. Their stench filled the decreasing space, which slowly ebbed away their resistance to disease and death. Side by side, throughout their never-ending journey, the living, near dying and dead, lay or propped each other up in their sailing vault.

I witness in their watery eyes, the joy of their approaching death, they smiled and rejoiced silently, at the knowledge that death would make them free once more. Then, they would return to their homelands, families and villages, that they had been so violently and brutally torn from. I accompanied my brothers and sisters, across the Atlantic Ocean in their pain and grief, in the hold of a galleon. In snatched moments, the folk stories of their homelands were whispered among them. The recollections of their heroes and heroines comforted and gave them hope.

"Anancy," they sighed silently and secretly.

My brothers and sisters recalled, how in their folk stories, the tiny spider could change into his human form and win battles against humans, animals and gigantic creatures. They hoped that I too might be among them, captured while in my human form. Like me, they wanted to win major battles, against the slave traders and the slave masters. Then, they would be able to return to their homelands and roam with their animals.

I watched again and again, as the cowardly captors' whips lashed out on the blistering and bleeding bodies of shackled men, women and children in their confined and diseased spaces. I intervened to help them win morale-boosting victories, against their cruel captors whenever possible.

"No more of your stupid noises, I want a quiet hold tonight. Your gods and Obeah people can't help you now," hissed the guard scornfully.

"I'll warn you all again, quiet tonight or you'll be thrown overboard."

They stared into the darkness that clothed them, lost in a world far, far away; a world the slave traders could not know or take from them.

"I must praise the spirit of my ancestors," I declared.

I chanted in Akan, Hausa, Igbo, Kikongo, Yoruba, the languages of their homelands, to the stifled smiles of my sisters and brothers. The darkness covered a sea of faces, as they erupted into broad grins of pleasure, to the fury of the guard.

"Defy me would you, you stupid and devilish Negro."

Changing back and forth from my human form to my spider shape, the guard's whip lashed out loud and urgent, to terrify and silence me and my kinfolk. I danced in and out of the strokes, exhausting as well as frightening our guard. Troubled by the actions of a chained African, he fled to the deck stuttering.

"A Negro freed himself. He was performing a savage dance to the others. I whipped him, but he just disappeared. When I turned around, there he was again, chanting and dancing to his ancestors and gods I swear."

Africans in the hold of a slave ship. Source Coelho. P (1981) Akapwitchi Akaporo, Armas e Escravos. Instituto Nacional Do Livro e do Disco, Maputo, Mozambique.

"I know," said the captain, "that these Blackies think they are special. I can assure you that these ideas are in their heads. If they were rare mortals, they would not be jam-packed in the hold of this galleon in their filth, stench and shackled together all five hundred of them."

"I think," he continued, "you have been on the 'rum' while on duty. This has made you delirious; you know the punishment for drinking rum on duty, twelve lashes of the cow's whip.

"No, no, I haven't," he wailed feebly.

The captain nodded. The lash of the cow's whip and the wailing of the guard reminded them of their fate if their captors believed they were communicating with each other, or with their ancestors.

I continued to entertain and soothe, my extended family members with my mischievous antics. I amused them with the playfulness of the forest animals, they had known in the storytelling gatherings, under broadly shading trees and around compound fires. I danced the Junkanoo dances of the different groups, playing the various parts. I carried out the traditional ceremonies, so dear to my chained sisters and brothers. I comforted, protected and defended them in any way I could.

Briefly, they fell into an intense slumber, to block out the horrors of the Atlantic crossing. They woke refreshed but still chained and shackled in the holds of tumbling galleons, away from their close families, friends and motherland. Those who survived the filth and contaminated ship's interiors and the never-ending sea journey; together they limped and stumbled into the clear, clean island sun. For a split second, they left behind the torture, pain and violence of the slave galleon.

The Africans blinked, stared and tried to take in their new surroundings. The lush foliage and beauty of the distant mountainous landscape, meeting the sea slapped their faces with the most refreshing strokes. They had woken from their nightmare. They had returned home. Soon they would be folded in the love and warmth of their families. They were free. They did not know then, that this was the beginning of a life of wandering. It was a journey that would take them throughout the centuries, further and further away from their motherland.

All of a sudden, red grizzly faces shattered their hopefulness. The planters and overseers scrutinised their newly arrived cargo. They were prodded and poked with cattle irons. They fell in agony, as the overseers' whips ate into their still tender and fragile flesh, starved of nourishing food and sunshine in the bowels of slave galleons. Agonising pain shot through their bodies. The red-hot irons, with the symbols of the plantations, sunk their sizzling, red scorched faces into their already fading flesh. The branding marks left on their buttocks, shoulders and faces, fixed their fate as an enslaved workforce, to be tracked and hunted if they left the plantations to regain their freedom.

The bonds of friendship and pain forged in the transatlantic crossing were once again ripped apart. They were scattered to plantations, on the islands and the mainland of South America. The overseers' whips silenced them. It also silenced the beautiful music of the brightly coloured birds and insects as they glided and fluttered through the wooded valleys and roaring rivers. The echoes of their whips reverberated across the shifting misty mountain peaks and hill chains, of these exquisite island paradises instead. In hours of never-ending labour, along with moments of respite, dreams and silent worlds, massaged away the pain of their tired and blistered limbs.

My mission was to ensure that our African heritage survived, the violence and destruction of the slave masters. They had banned the family, languages, dress, music, religion and traditions of our motherland. From dawn to dusk, the Africans' only entitlement from their endless labour was to grow food on their meagre house plots and on distant provision grounds to feed themselves. Sunday was their only full day of rest and renewal, away from the planters' cane pieces.

My antics fleetingly eased their pain. I changed from man to spider, to help them gain victories of varying degrees, against the powerful and contemptible planters and their employees. Spinning webs high in the tallest trees, I became a spy, I warned the napping workers of the stealthy approach, of the drivers and overseers. At other times, I spun a springy web that entangled the feet of the horses and sent them headlong into ditches and thorny hedges, the hidden smiles of my kinfolk, was a satisfying reward. I carried messages between the plantations, learning the languages of the different Ethnic groups. I made it my duty to know their desires and innermost thoughts, as well as their yearning to make their homes, in the sapphire layered mountains, hills and forests that resembled their motherland. Along with their fiery zeal, to end the monstrous regime of slavery.

Obsessively, I listened to news spoken in muted voices, from far off places knowing it might contain information that would help us. I listened and shared it with my brothers and sisters. I looked out from my web high in the towering trees and saw the red-coated armies in search of them. I intervened, giving the runaways and rebels, time to attack and retreat to safety. Swiftly, they fled to freedom in the shimmering hills, mountains and forests areas of these breath-taking islands and the mainland. High in my web, with the slave masters' plans fixed in my memory, I took it to the African resistance, seeking their freedom.

CHAPTER 3

The source

Occasionally, the tranquillity of our self-sufficient villages and compounds were disturbed by events beyond their boundaries. Curiously, the population raised their heads and looked in the direction of the commotion. Assured that it was just another of the little niggles, that were a feature of everyday life; promptly they returned to their domestic and regular routines. They cultivated their extensive maize and millet fields, as well as looking after their animals. During the harvest months, they stored their abundant crops for when the life-giving rain ceased for long periods and threatened their existence.

Their daily routine created the most productive and cooperative communities. These communal relationships grew over time, based on the family as well as strong religious practices, grounded in centuries of traditions. Our traditions had served the ancestors well. We would continue in these tried and tested ways of living, organising and working co-operatively to improve our communities, thus securing everyone's future.

Suddenly, in a very short time, our taken for granted and everyday routines, were shattered by forces we did not fully understand. These forces and people had very quietly and slyly crept upon, our composed and well-ordered compounds and villages. They almost tore them apart. They snatched many of our industrious inhabitants, going about their ordinary routines. They kidnapped them and carted them off to far off shores. Anxiously, our fretful compounds and villages watched for these vile intruders. Thieves who would seize their family members, thus ending their precious family and communal life.

A domestic scene in an African village before the European incursion. Source Coelho. P (1981) Akapwitchi Akaporo, Armas e Escravos. Instituto Nacional Do Livro e do Disco. Maputo, Mozambique.

Imagine the tormented families and compounds, as my kinfolk wept and pined for their stolen family members. Passionately, they guarded their remaining relatives and friends, from the despicable thieves. We had to find the source, of the turmoil that was ripping apart, our beloved motherland. Tirelessly, I defended my brothers and sisters, who were about to be taken. Repeatedly, I challenged the vile human thieves. However, the scoundrels lurked in every corner of our compounds and villages. We could not purge our countryside or continent of them.

Vigorously, my brothers and sisters had resisted their capture and confinement too. Unfortunately, very few had returned to tell of their ordeal and those who were responsible for their disappearance. I, Anancy, man and spider took up the challenge, to seek the source of the despair and devastation that was upon us. The escalating theft of our people would destroy us. Collectively, as Africans we had to confront and end it.

Dear reader, I must take you back in time, to the origins of our anguish and grief. Come with me, as I cross the Atlantic Ocean, lodged in a floating log, transported by colossal tidal waves and currents. These tidal waves, rage and soar from Africa's West coast, before dumping their gushing torrents on the islands and the mainland of the Americas, during the sweltering months, of the hurricane season.

The receding waves of the tropical storm fizzled out onto a distant continent, it tossed me onto Mexico's Eastern shoreline. As I explored and familiarised myself with the extensive landscape around me, I stumbled on some huge carved heads, with the facial features of Africa. I was amazed and puzzled, but curious and extremely proud of these representations of my ancestors', distinguished past. My ancestors must have made this journey long, long ago. They must have been avid explorers and merchants. They had crossed the Atlantic Ocean centuries ago in their robust sailing ships. These enormous and sculptured African faces welcomed me, I felt at home.

Intrigued, I explored the images. I imagined a glorious African past when our ancestors traded with the ancient peoples of the world in freedom. Subsequently, they had settled and farmed these rich and fertile lands, as they had done in their homelands. The traditions of their motherland had guided them in everything they did. They had only taken what they needed from the land. They had preserved this mineral rich and fertile landscape, for those who would come after them. The ancestors had left these enormous tokens of themselves, as well as some of their traditions and their presence to link the Americas and Africa's shared past.

Inspired and reassured by my ancestors' sojourn of long, long, ago, eagerly I explored the stunning civilisations of the Amerindian peoples. These towered and nestled on and between the vertical and fertile mountainsides above me. I wanted to and needed to learn about this magnificent and hospitable continent, along with the great civilisations it had nurtured and was still nurturing.

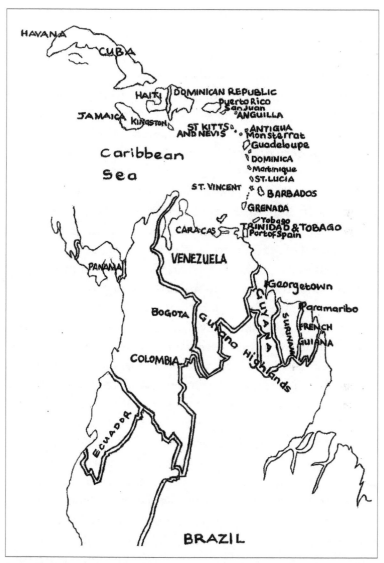

A drawing of the islands and mainland countries along the Caribbean coast of South America.

The intricate architectural structures situated on the mountains enticed me to examine the multitude of buildings and dwelling places that were carved high upon the ascending rock faces, looking down on the plains. These magnificent valleys of pyramids, with their pristine and elaborate detailing, displayed the skill and aptitude of the master craftsmen, as well as their artisan workforce over time. If my ancestors had left towering images of themselves, on the South American mainland, the subsequent civilisations would also leave behind their magnificent treasures too. The substantial, detailed and intricately sculptured stone structures, valleys of pyramids and ingenious agricultural formations, amazed and left me in awe of their genius, dexterity and accomplishments.

As I explored these dazzling examples of the Amerindians' past, I was struck by the ornate gold sun faces and decorations. These lined the inner chambers of their palaces, pyramids and temples. These intricate gold sun faces, delicately carved people, animals and objects on the shrines and altars; demonstrated their respect and worship of the powerful forces all around them. The gold sun faces mirrored nature's most powerful force, the sun, the source of their lives and our lives too.

I reflected on the similarities, between the peoples of my motherland across the ocean and the inhabitants of the South American mainland. Now, I fully understood, why my ancestors, had settled on this mineral rich and bountiful continent. They had left images from their homeland, on the mainland.

In the distance, the miniature mounds jutting out of the wavy ocean above the coastline drew me forcibly towards their shores, as well as the secrets within their undulating terrain. Spinning a rugged thread, I descended and exited the splendour of the mainland and the Amerindian peoples' golden past and present. Speeding through time yet again, I am impatient to meet and understand the forces, which would devastate these hospitable and inventive peoples, as well as plundering their mineral rich and fertile continent.

My spider eyes dart about for transport, to the hilly and mountainous mounds protruding from the ocean's depths, as they pull me towards their shores. My transport had waited for me. The trading rafts and canoes, basked in the sun with their bulky cargoes, waiting to journey across the high seas. I hitched a ride in one of their gigantic sails. The chain of islands drew me towards their steamy interior, gushing torrents, rising pinnacles and wooded landscape.

Further afield, the diligent and miniature people with their shiny black hair, velvety brown skins and sparkling dark eyes, work and fade from my view as night covers the land and sea. Unceremoniously, again my transport flung itself onto the night shore, now partially illuminated by a crescent moon. Quickly, the inhabitants haul the life-giving salt baskets off the rafts and canoes. They refilled them with stacks of the salted and smoked bodies of the wild boars that had roamed the emerald mountains. I exited my transport, as it prepared for its speedy return across the dusky ocean with its delicacy.

I withdrew to the dark, spidery places until the rays of the golden sun rose and lit up the raging sea. Slowly, it breathed life and industry into the workers, as well as the hazy and extensive mountain peaks of the island. I emerged from the dark interiors, to explore the fishy coastline that buzzed with frantic activity. The small sailing dugouts, bobbed up and down on the pounding sea, as the fishermen and boys retrieved their catch or replaced their baskets and nets.

Moving closer to the industrious coastline, the fish and turtle beds are meticulously looked after by the fishermen and their assistants. The seagulls screamed and dived onto the shore, to take their share of the fishermen's catch. The enormous waves crashed onto the shore and covered the boys, as they plunged into them, leaving their nets idly on the seashore. In contrast, the women and girls dragged sacks of drying fish, carefully they stacked them in the sun on rickety platforms while their pungent aroma tainted the fresh sea air.

Exhausted but delighted, by the extensive and industrious coastal seascapes, I am automatically, drawn to the highlands as well as the valleys beneath them. In the distance, the Yucca or Cassava plants with their spindly trunks and mass of pea-green leaves at their crown covered the plains. Tenderly, they are weeded, and the soil around their roots is built up, by the nimble fingers of the women and children. Beyond the Yucca fields, the trailing vines of the sweet potatoes, cocoyams and squash plants stretched into the distance. Seamlessly, their boundaries merged with the extensive maize and cotton fields, covering the island's terrain.

In the interior, of these vast lands, the miniature multi-coloured peppers of the chilli pepper plant sparkled and glittered in the sun. The cocoa pods pulled their branches towards the soil, in readiness to be harvested, roasted and consumed. Excited, but worn out by my journey of discovery, I spun a steely web into a nearby Guava tree. I reflected once again, on the similarities of this and the African landscape. Presently, the stillness of the forest's interior carried me off into an intense and restful sleep; as the gigantic heads of my ancestors on the mainland returned again and again to my consciousness.

The night orchestra shrieked and screamed, as their nocturnal slumber was shattered, by the silent but nimble feet of the Taino patrols. They hastened to the shore in great numbers, to monitor the ghost-like vessels, approaching the coastline. Violently, my web vibrates almost casting me, into the thick undergrowth. The twinkling fireflies guide my sleepy eyes in the black night, towards the turmoil offshore, where the skeleton of three large and eerie vessels, formed part of an ominous night sky.

The dancing flames of their torches illuminated the shadowy coastline. The scouts and soldiers of the Taino people watched anxiously to ascertain the intentions of the mirage approaching their coast. Jerkily, the strange vessels moved along in the dim moonlight. They tilted and swayed in the motionless night sea as if they were piloting themselves. They drifted and turned sharply until the hush and tranquillity of the night ceased abruptly. The hardened wood of the Santa Maria, flung herself onto the hard rocky boulders, above and beneath the coastline. Insects and small creatures scurried to safety under rocks and crevasses.

The bewildered Taino Cacique and his soldiers prepared to defend their coastline from the unexpected intrusion. The ghostlike white crew crawled out of the half-wrecked craft. They waddled towards the two lilting, but upright vessels nearby. Anxiously, we all waited and waited; however, the galleons and their crew, remained a fantasy off the shoreline, until daylight.

The sun rose, it breathed life into the stranded galleons and their occupants. The bearded white-faced sailors emerged from their stricken transport onto small rafts. The rafts bobbed up and down and sailed towards the shore. The straight-haired and bronzed Taino people retreated into the foliage around their coastline. They prepared themselves for an encounter, with divinities, their folklore and myths, had warned would come among them one day.

The gentle and hospitable Taino people and their army prepared to defend their territory; as the bedraggled and demoralised Spanish crew and their commander lurched themselves fearfully towards Ayiti's shore. Desperate and hungry, Columbus stumbled onto the grains of golden sand, waving a white flag as a symbol of his friendliness. His men waited in trepidation at the water's edge. Anxiously, he approached the gentle and generous Taino army and Cacique. Inquisitively, they scrutinised the visitor before them, he was unlike anything they had seen before.

A smile forced its way across Columbus' pale and part wrinkled face; his outstretched hand full of shiny and glittery beads. The Taino army aimed their clubs and spears at his heart. The stand–off continued for what seemed like an eternity, until the Cacique surrounded by his army and advisors, gave way to the hospitality of his homeland. He instructed his people, to give their visitor a warm and hearty Taino welcome.

Relieved and smiling, Columbus stretched out his hands once more, with the trifling gifts he had brought from Spain. Slowly, a broad smile crept across his face, as he tried to convey to the Cacique and the Taino people, his goodwill. A shell trumpet blew, and hundreds of Taino soldiers and the populace surrounded the lone visitor. When he was confident that their lone visitor was of no immediate threat to himself and his people; the

Cacique ordered refreshments for his guest. Promptly, a banquet was laid out under a sprawling Silk Cotton tree nearby. They would keep him out of their villages and holy places until they had consulted the spirits, gods and their ancestors.

The smell of freshly baked Cassava bread and seafood, simmered in chilli pepper sauce, floated along the coastline. Columbus salivated and gladly accepted the Cacique's generosity to partake in the feast. Ravenously, he filled his protruding stomach, as he continued to smile graciously at his hosts.

At the end of the meal, the Cacique bade him farewell. He ordered his men, to make a comfortable reed house for their guest, to spend the rest of the day and night. He headed for their sacred shrine, with his assembled courtiers and advisors, to ask the powerful spirits and gods, for guidance on the night's events.

Disappointed, Columbus remained in isolation and wondered about the glittering gold headdress and pendants, around the necks of the Cacique and his courtiers. He comforted himself that he had achieved the goals he had set for himself. This bold navigator had reached the Indies, by sailing west. The King and Queen of Spain would be pleased; they had had, faith in his plans to sail west to get to the Indies. They had financed this eventful journey. Columbus reflected on the fact that the King of Portugal had laughed at his plans. They had blocked his attempts, to sail south. He had triumphed over all of them and would present the Spanish monarchs, with all the spices they needed, plus his new found discovery, gold. This intrepid Commander would re-negotiate, another five percent on his ten percent commission, for his additional and valuable cargo, gold.

As he lay in his reed house, waiting for his hosts that evening, he plotted how he would get his hands on the gold jewellery; that adorned the slender but muscular bodies of the Taino males and the island for his King and country. He bowed humbly to them and displayed his most endearing smile. Columbus made it plain to them his love of the beautiful jewellery they wore on their bodies. The Commander had to restrain himself, from grabbing the gold from their person. Then he signalled to them, in the most non-interested manner, his interest in their gold jewellery.

The Cacique offered to send him, some gold pieces the next day as a gift. He was impressed with his gestures of eloquence and praise of their sacred gold medallions. That night Columbus could not sleep; he tossed and turned thinking about the gold ingots he would get the next day. The ageing Italian explorer began to plot how to get to the source of the treasure and received the gold nuggets with the utmost modesty. He indicated to the messenger that he wanted to know where on the island it had come from. Unable, to communicate with Columbus, who did not understand or speak Arawakan, the messenger left the gold and returned to the Cacique.

At their next meeting, Columbus demonstrated to the Cacique that he was going to see how the work was getting on, to re-float his wrecked galleon, the Santa Maria. He mimed that he wanted more pieces of gold to take with him, the Cacique agreed. Next morning, as the sun rose, Columbus left the island and waded out to his stranded vessels, clutching the pieces of gold. His men rushed to tell him that the Santa Maria had sunk; he shoved them aside and called his officers together. He showed them only a few pieces of the nuggets. They were amazed and asked him where it had come from. Columbus told them that the island was full of precious metals; the population wore gold as if it were shells on the seashore.

Next, Columbus informed them that the island now belonged to the monarchs of Spain, only the Cacique and his people did not know it yet. They needed only fifty men to take the whole island. The inhabitants were childlike and heathens; they worshipped many gods and the strangest objects. He had to save their souls; they must be converted to Catholicism as soon as possible. The Commander reassured his crew that the Cacique and his people would accept the King and Queen of Spain's rule over them; when he was in total control of the island. The gold on the island belonged to the Spanish monarchs.

The Chief informed his officers of his forthcoming plans. He intended to take some Taino people to Spain to learn their language, Arawakan and show the king his new subjects. They would make excellent servants at the court. He would also take the cotton and the gold they had been forced to dig out of the ground for him. The Navigator would describe to the King and Queen their new colony Hispaniola, which looked so much like Spain, he had named it little Spain. When Columbus returned a year later, with a fleet of galleons, soldiers and weapons to assert his total control over the entire island; the Taino people had massacred his men. He had instructed them, to enslave the people and make them build forts, dig gold and silver from the mines, as well as growing cotton.

Unfortunately, for the Taino people, Columbus' enlarged arsenal and army weakened their fearless resistance, to the invasion of their motherland. They were determined to rid their homeland of the invaders, so many of them fled to the craggy and dense mountain peaks with their Caciques, to drive them from their island. Gradually their resistance, to the Spanish occupation of their motherland, was hindered, by the diseases brought by the invaders, which almost wiped out their population and society.

Twenty-five years after Columbus staggered onto the island of Ayiti, the land of mountains, the Taino people were very near to extinction. This is where my story, our story begins.

CHAPTER 4

The greatest land grab of all time and its consequences

Columbus' reckless shipwreck in December 1492 on Ayiti's rocky coastline, had dire repercussions for the highly developed and thriving Taino and Amerindian peoples. It had consequences for their civilisation as well as the entire region and beyond. The theft of the island and region's gold and silver, along with the enslavement and the near extinction of its population, created a demand for another substantial and unpaid workforce. Heartlessly, the Spanish priest and colonist Bartholomew de Las Casas, a passionate champion of free labour, advised his King to replace the declining Taino population, with Africans, in his stolen lands.

In 1493, Pope Alexander VI settled the claims of Portugal and Spain for the lands they claimed, they had discovered outside Europe, during their voyages of exploration. He divided the islands and the mainland of South America, between Spain and Portugal, to the exclusion of the other European countries. Portugal got Brazil and the exclusive rights to the West African Coast. Spain got the islands and the mainland of South America.

At the end of the 15th, Century and the beginning of the 16th Century, when my brothers and sisters were landed on Ayiti under coercion, some fled to the mountains. They met groups of Taino people and their Caciques resisting the Spanish invaders. Forced to seek sanctuary in the mountains of their homeland; the Taino people had continued to resist the Spanish invaders and their administration.

However, the majority of Africans replaced the Taino people, mining gold and silver, on the mineral-rich islands of Ayiti and

Puerto Rico. Unfortunately, for the Taino people, on the nearby islands of Xaymaca, Cuba and Trinidad, the minor deposits of gold under their soil, did not save them from enslavement and subsequent destruction. They too were enslaved and were worked to death growing tobacco, cassava and cotton. Many were forced to herd cattle, to supply the invaders with provision and equipment, for their exploration of the rest of the South American mainland. They too resisted their enslavement. Naturally, they fled into the mountainous landscape of Jamaica, Cuba and Trinidad, where they fought the Spanish, to recover their motherland.

As more and more, of my brothers and sisters were forcibly landed on these islands, some of them joined the Taino people in their mountainous enclaves across the islands, to be free and self-directing. Having no other option, but to live in the marginal and rocky landscape of Jamaica, the Taino people and later the Africans, used the foothills as their hunting grounds, farmlands and pathways across the island. The rich and fertile coastal lands, of the Taino people, had been stolen from them. Now, they were hunted down and enslaved if they left their rocky and sparse homes in search of food.

In the meantime, Britain, France and The Netherlands looked on as the Spanish and Portuguese Kings and their nobility rebuilt their countries; from the mined gold and silver taken from The Enslaved World. These monarchs were green with envy. They encouraged and gave permission to desperadoes, such as pirates from Britain and buccaneers from France; to steal the gold and silver from the galleons, as they sailed to Spain and Portugal. Francis Drake and Captain Morgan were some of the pirates who operated in the ocean and the seas. Captain Morgan raided Spanish colonies and their sailing convoys and stole gold and silver. Much later, he became governor of Jamaica for a short while. Eventually, these priceless minerals were dug out of the ground.

Years later, the other European monarchs looked enviously, at the vast and fertile lands, stolen and cultivated by, the Spanish

Spanish/British Administrative Building from 1534 in Spanish Town (St Jago de la Vega), Jamaica.

and Portuguese. Again, they used pirates and buccaneers, to mount periodic attacks off their shores, to capture them. They wanted to make money from the crops; the Portuguese and Spanish now grew on the islands and mainland, sugar. Sugar had become a very high priced commodity in Europe. It was sought after, because of the huge profits that could be made from growing and processing it. Sugar was so expensive at the time that only the very wealthy could afford it. Household servants were carefully supervised when this costly commodity was taken from locked pantries, to be added to the family's meal.

In 1655, the British army and pirates were sent to capture Spain's riches and best-defended sugar island, Hispaniola. The Spanish army repelled them forcefully and so, they took Jamaica instead. The majority of the Spanish army and settlers fled to Cuba and Hispaniola. However, a small group of settlers, along with the governor-general and their African allies, fled into the mountains and fought for many years to drive out the new invaders.

They Spanish and African resistance fighters waged war on the early British planters, as soon as they began to farm very close to their hunting and farming lands, in the foothills. The

Spanish soldiers and settlers, that had fled to Hispaniola and Cuba, intended to retake their island. To keep the Spanish and the other European countries out and defend the island; the British government gave many incentives, to encourage British people to quickly settle on the island and set up sugar plantations.

Soon, the theft and shipment of my brothers and sisters, from across our motherland soared. They laboured unceasingly on the emerging sugar plantations, which were rapidly being set up on the island. I, my fellow Africans as well as the Taino people in the mountaintops, continued to resist the threat to our survival forcefully. They had no choice, but to continue to hunt in the lands around the foothills, to feed themselves and their families. Conflict with the new planters escalated. The colonists intended to drive them, from the stony mountains and enslave them, to work on their newly acquired plantations. Naturally, the Taino and African peoples fought to retain their freedom, in their mountainous sanctuaries across the island. These mountain refuges would provide safe havens for their newly arriving brothers and sisters, escaping from the violence of plantation slavery.

Initially, the Spanish invaders had only settled on the larger islands; they extracted gold, silver, and pearls and much later they grew sugar. The other European nations and their pirate adventurers had no other option but to settle on the remaining islands. They settled on the islands of Antigua, the Bahamas, Barbados, Bermuda, Grenada, Guadeloupe, Martinique, Nevis, St Kitts and the remaining islands. British settlers from Barbados and Nevis were encouraged and given land to set up plantations, in Jamaica, their most recent and biggest colony.

One such planter was a Mr Bax. He had set up his first sugar plantation in Barbados, which he called Bax Hall. He employed an agent and an overseer to find him suitable land to cultivate sugar in Jamaica. He intended to expand his fortune and influence in the islands, but especially at home in Britain. Subsequently, a significant number of persons from the British nobility and others rushed to acquire the most fertile coastal

Spanish/British building in Spanish Town Square, Jamaica.

lands. They set up plantations, on as many islands and the mainland as they could afford.

I divided my time, equally between the grand dwellings of the planters and the hellish shacks of my family, on the hillocks a few miles away. I needed to be in both places, I was the link between them. Bax Hall, which he later named after his plantation in Barbados, was previously owned by one of the many absentee planters on the islands and the mainland. These planters had no desire to live in the tropics. They preferred to live in their stately homes in England, while the enslaved Africans financed their luxurious lifestyles, growing the 'golden' sugarcane. Their agents and overseers managed their plantations in their absence.

Frequently, they were poor whites, some were Irish prisoners captured during the many wars with the British army and sold and transported to work on the plantations. Others were abducted and transported for minor debts or offences. These persons usually served seven years as indentured servants, working for the planters, for food and lodgings only. Their poor health to begin with, hard work, the climate and diseases, meant that many had died at the end of seven years. The remainder had become pirates and petty traders while the rest were free but penniless.

Enviously, the agents and overseers looked at the enormous wealth they were forcing the enslaved Africans to create for their masters. They too wanted to own plantations and Africans. They too dreamt of returning to England, with great fortunes, power and influence. They took their opportunity. They worked my brothers and sisters to near death, to get their share from the plantations. They made sure that their rations were just enough to give them the strength, to return to the cane pieces each morning. The remainder, they sold to finance their dreams of becoming wealthy and successful planters.

The enslaved Africans were given four ounces of dried salted fish, a few ounces of salted pig's tail, half a sack of guinea corn and molasses for households of four or more. The agents and overseers provided just enough land for the families to build the smallest of wattle and daub houses. They grew vegetables, on the outer edges of their little rocky plots, to supplement their meagre diet. They also produced food, on their shared provision grounds, in the hills.

The agents and overseers put into practice, another of their plans to enrich themselves. They took significant amounts of food produced by the enslaved Africans; and sold it to increase their miserable wages. This intensified the brutal system of slavery. Unsurprisingly, the agent and overseer spent almost nothing on maintaining the plantation. It deteriorated, as the ponds dug to catch water, ran dry during the recurring dry seasons. They did not seek to find, other ways to secure water supplies for the plantation. Dramatically, cane production fell on this plantation in these years. My family members were forced to share the same water with the animals, many died from diseases. I watched my people die needlessly.

The strongest of them fled to the mountains using the over the hills and mountain railroad. They were welcomed once again by the Taino people, along with the descendants of the African-

Spanish Maroons in the mountains. Others wandered onto plantations, where they could get food at the end of a hard day's work.

Fresh from his small but imposing estate and Jacobean style house in Barbados; Mr Bax had many new ideas for this his first plantation in Jamaica. He needed money to live in the style of the planter he had bought the estate from. He had plans to buy or build a stately home, in a shire county in England, as soon as he had enough money. Mr Bax remodelled the bedraggled plantation, to get the maximum production from sugarcane cultivation, as well as hefty returns on his spending.

Mr Bax made sure the plantation would have enough water, to ensure production, even in times of severe drought. He instructed the African craftsmen, to build a water wheel, using water from the nearby river. These changes dramatically increased sugar production. He provided for the basic needs of the enslaved Africans because it would ensure enormous returns on his investments. Before returning to Barbados, he personally supervised the renovation of the plantation.

I watched and admired the skill of the African craftsmen. They knocked down the old mud houses, replacing them with new stone houses. Six new compounds were built, each housing fifty African households. They were built on the edge of the plantation, above the cane pieces and a considerable distance from the planter's house. The outbuildings were placed close to the channels that brought water to the new water wheel on the plantation. Three hundred Africans now worked the six hundred acre estate. They worked to secure its smooth running, but most of all to ensure a high-quality lifestyle as well as substantial returns on his money for Mr Bax.

The former house plots were used as provision grounds to grow food and wood, to supplement their rations. A small hut was built to serve as a hot or sick house. It was used for those mutilated by the overseers and drivers' whips. It was small and pokey to make sure they would not spend too much time there; it worked. They continued to use the traditional medicines of the matrons and medicine people in the fresh air under huge Guango and Silk Cotton trees. I delighted in collecting lime, the bark of the bitter tree and I also grew and stored other medicinal plants, I knew and used in Africa. I mixed potions to ward off the deadly malaria, yellow fever, yaws and running bellies.

A stone building was constructed as a schoolroom. Again, as you would imagine, not much took place there, as children from their earliest years had to pick among the bundles of cane, to reach Mr Bax's and his overseers' targets. The older children were too busy at work in the cane pieces, mills, distillery, storerooms and animal pens to go to school. A church was built within walking distance of the plantation house. In their high and mighty churches, they thanked their God for giving them the opportunity, to exploit men, women and children without mercy from dawn to dusk, six days a week. Passages from their holy book justified the enslavement of the Taino and later the African peoples.

Those Africans who accompanied them to church, on Sunday, after Sunday held the prayer and hymn books open for them. They learnt the words that they were forbidden to read and use to improve themselves. Secretly, they passed it on to their fellow Africans, without the planters knowing. They would one day become the lay preachers, who would incite their congregations, to rise up against the inhumanity of slavery and end it.

The natural skill of the African carpenters, stone masons and tradespeople revamped the plantation yard. The craftsmen ensured that the farm machinery and production would be maintained for the sole use of Mr Bax and his heirs. A few water holes were dug, to provide water for the precious animals in times of extreme drought. Wooden boats made up a small fleet that supplied the plantation with fish. The best seafood for the planter's table – the tail, head, fins and sprats – was dried and salted and kept in the storerooms for the enslaved workforce.

The changes on the plantation marginally benefited them, but it also squeezed from them the maximum labour for their owner. Mr Bax in keeping with his fellow planters and the plantation system did not pay them for their work; even though he considered himself an 'enlightened and model plantation owner'. Mothers had to return to the cane pieces, directly after giving birth. Their children nestled in the cooler corners of the cane pieces or secured on their backs in the first few weeks. The aged and disabled continued to work on the plantation, milling, sifting, bagging and bottling, the cane products. The frail and helpless managed as best as they could. Thus, their life span was brutally shortened, by excessive work, an inadequate diet, beatings, rape and a host of violent punishments.

The planters had calculated that working the Africans to death over a short period of time would get them the maximum returns from their investments. They could easily buy more of them, from the slave traders, who competed to supply slaves from across the continent at competitive prices. The vast profits from growing sugar and other crops stimulated the never-ending demand for their labour on the plantations. It fuelled the rocketing trade in human beings from the African continent and the phenomenal growth of sugar and other plantations on the islands and the mainland of South America.

The constant uprisings, by my family members, were curtailed by the continuous repopulating and movement of them and their families, between the plantations on the islands and the mainland. My family worked from sunrise to sunset. I could not remove their tough and grinding labours, except aid them when I could. I used my antics to make them smile their unseen smiles or deflect some of the oppressive blows of the overseers and drivers. My brothers and sisters laboured excessively, except for the unborn babies and me.

My vision, our vision and goal, were to end the slave trade and plantation slavery by whatever means. Our ambition was the return to our motherland, for all those who wanted it. It preoccupied my sleeping and waking hours. Our work, as well as my mission, was endless.

CHAPTER 5

Bax Hall sugar plantation

Bax Hall sugar plantation was and is still situated in the parish of St Ann. It is close to one of the places, where Columbus drifted onto the island in 1494, a place the Spanish renamed New Seville. It was not the biggest plantation on the island, but many enslaved Africans started their life of back-breaking labour there. It is bordered, by the crystal clear Caribbean Sea to the North, with its inlets, coves and sandy beaches. The rolling hill peaks, mountains and meadows of the Northern parishes framed its Southern boundary.

I roamed the wooded hills and mountain pinnacles, hidden by the gliding mist framing the North coast of Jamaica, the land of wood and water. I skirted the perpendicular mountainsides, covered with thick vegetation. I explored the cool subterranean caves and burrowed deep under the white sandy beaches; in search of secret places to conceal Africans. Africans fleeing from the barbaric white planters, overseers and drivers, on plantations across the island. These hidden places proved invaluable meeting places for the rebel Africans. I observed, listened and learnt how to defeat the monstrous regime of slavery, while my people laboured continuously under the threat of the cow's whip.

Slowly, the chill morning mist drifted across the plantation yard, with its array of buildings, forcing the daily routine to begin. The planter's house stood in an elevated position, to catch the ocean breeze. At a respectable distance, stood the mill, boiling and still houses, storerooms, workshops, stables and animal pens. Daily, they wore away the youth and life of my relations. In the distance hillocks, the crowded dwellings of my kinfolk crouched on the tiniest of plots. They looked down on the sweltering cane pieces. From these patches of rocks, they eked out food which barely fed and sustained them, after their grinding labour in the cane pieces.

The sun squeezed through the tiny cracks in the walls and makeshift openings. It exposed many squashed bodies, sleeping on thick mud floors. The thatched plantain leaves rustled on the roofs, as the chilly morning breeze glided slowly across the yard; compelling my people to rise and face, another day of back-breaking labour, in the cane pieces.

Kindling fires uncover shadows, sipping bush tea from calabash bowls. Teas brewed by ancient African matrons, too old to work in the cane pieces now. These teas and medicinal shrubs would strengthen and protect their bodies, from the hazards of the murky cane pieces, as well as the sting of the overseer's whip. Effortlessly, silhouettes move among the vegetables and small bushes, perched precariously on the edges of miniature house plots. On the edges of these rocky plots, their food was lovingly grown, to supplement their meagre rations, during their few hours of relief.

The shrouded figures trudge mechanically towards the cane piece. The whirring wheels of the horse carts and mill turn in unison and gathered speed in readiness, for the fruits of their labour. Small creatures such as mice, snakes, frogs, cane piece rats, crabs, as well as wriggling creatures scurry to safety. Rapidly, they flee as the swish of the cutlasses, and the hard, cracked feet of my enslaved brothers and sisters moved through the cane pieces instinctively. Skilfully, and confidently, they weeded, cut, planted and reaped the sugarcane during its rigorous yearly cycle.

The thud of cane landing on the open ground roused them, especially the incapacitated and very young, into feverish action. The whip of the wrinkled sun dried overseer whizzed and sliced the stifling heat above the scorching cane piece. Then, it curled and lashed out again and again. It dug into the flesh of a young lad without warning. It struck out a second time; blood erupted and trickled across his bent torso. He stumbled but forced himself up to continue his work as the glint in the eye of the overseer told him his sadistic intentions.

Nyerere, the cart driver, moved quickly to aid his family, as the cane was bundled and thrown into the wagon. Swiftly, the others work not to attract, the recurring lash of the brute's whip.

"Faster, faster," the beast barked.

Then, the tyrannical whip lashed out again. This time onto the back of another disabled youth, tossing bundles of sugarcane into the cart. Briskly, bundles landed in the cart, as my people tried to avoid the sting of the whip. The injured youth bent to take another bundle of the cane. However, he toppled over as he threw it into the cart. Recklessly, the whip lashed out over and over again, into the maimed lad curled on the red earth, saturated daily with the blood of Africans. The mutilated boy raised his eyes to plead for mercy. His pleading eyes offended the barbarian. Furiously, he whipped the human bundle again and again; it oozed blood as it stiffened and stopped moving. Satisfied, the beast glared and whizzed his whip, at the Africans in the field. He raced to the next cane piece, in search of more defenceless victims.

The bundle lay in the blazing sun. I bathed his wounds again and again with soothing herbs infused in water. His eyes flickered now and again, but he did not recognise me, his helper. The labouring workers in the cane piece prayed and begged the gods of the earth, the wind, the sun and their ancestors, to take him into their loving care and end his wretchedness. They dared not break their labour; the brute had made his intention very clear.

Speedily, bundles of the cane landed on the cart, it heaved under the weight. Cart driver, Nyerere hurried towards the plantation yard storehouse. The bundle lay in the midday sun, the shadows of the afternoon and the cool of the evening as the sun set. Cart driver, Nyerere returned at dusk, his time was now his own. Angrily, he lifted and put the soaking bundle of blood into the cart and rushed to the matron's hut. Quickly, she massaged the almost lifeless body, with the herbs and poultices that she used daily, to ease the pain and revive the bodies of her people, mutilated by the overseers and drivers' whips.

Daily, the overseers' whips tore into their delicate flesh, to extract every ounce of labour from them. It also intended to rip from their consciousness, every aspect of their culture, language and identity, as peoples from across the African continent. The whip aimed to force into their consciousness instead, the slave master's malicious perceptions and descriptions of them, as lazy savages, devious, dishonest, dull and devoid of any culture, civilisation or humanity.

Vigorously, the enslaved Africans rejected the planters' description of them; they named themselves. They used the name the slave owners refused to use: Africans, the name of the continent that had reared them and from which they had been so brutally stolen. They were taken from across the African continent, and, therefore, spoke many different languages and dialects. They had numerous cultural practices and traditions. These were reflected in their belief systems, food, stories, dances, cuisines, styles of dress and many forms of recreation.

However, on the plantations of 'The Recently Enslaved World' their collective enslavement and the overseers' whips united them. It bonded them positively as Africans, from across the mineral rich, fertile and productive African continent. Likewise, they used some of the shared words, in their many languages and dialects to unify themselves. They also used their mother tongues, to disparagingly, name the white slave masters and their henchmen, the Backra. Their Anancy stories mocked and sabotaged the planters' craving to make plantation slavery the only option on the landscape of the world. Under the vigilant eye of the planters and their overseers, they used their Anancy stories to communicate. They used these stories to belittle them while grinding away at the system to retake their freedom.

My story, our story, is about enslaved Africans, from across the length and breadth of the vast African continent. Africans with a shared belief in our ancestors, the power of the forces in the natural world, varied cultural practices, as well as the beliefs and traditions which valued and celebrated all our humanity. Collectively, we would recreate and restore the humanity which had been ripped out of the islands and the mainland by the planters and their governments' greed and ruthlessness.

CHAPTER 6

Cudjoe

Our narrative is one of warfare and sacrifice, carried out by weaponless and constrained peoples from the African continent. The slave galleons that brought Africans, to 'The Recently Enslaved World' had in their bellies the ferocious warriors and leaders from the Akan, Bakongo, Coromanti, Ga, Ibo, Yoruba and other ethnic groups. These men, women, and children that were forcibly taken and shipped to the enslaved world fought fiercely to free themselves, from the moment they fell into the enslaver's trap.

Daily, they fled from the coastal and inland plantations to create their homelands, in the rocky blue-grey mist covered hills, mountains and deep wooded valleys of the islands and the mainland. On the plantations, the secret societies of Africa were rooted in the compounds, cane pieces and the big house. I, Anancy, man and spider, was the link between them. Day by day, the enslaved Africans laboured in the cane pieces, but they also worked unceasingly to secure routes out, of the plantations to free and sustainable lives.

"These plants and herbs are indispensable in our homelands; the medicine people used them to care for the people. Today, we also have to be thankful to our brothers and sisters, the Taino people. They have taught us so much about the medicinal foods, plants and herbs, that grow naturally on this island and the mainland. They have also taught us how to use them efficiently and effectively. Now, the medicine people are our only hope if we are to survive the dire consequences of our enslavement. They have passed down to us through the generations, the knowledge of the natural world, to enable us as a people to care for ourselves, reproduce and populate our dwelling places. When you see these plants and herbs, collect, dry and store them and make sure you know how to use them," Lumumba, the old warrior advised his son.

"Yes father, I've not seen these before, they don't grow in our compound."

"No, they grow in places that are cool and have a constant supply of water. These craggy and compacted limestone landscapes and caves have rich sources of plants and wild food. They are good hiding places for our weapons and soldiers when the planters' armies come after us. You must learn and master, the nook and crannies of these unique hill and mountain formations. Mark my words, very soon our survival and victory against the slave masters and their armies; will depend on you knowing and using these hiding places wisely," warned Lumumba, the old warrior.

As soon as, he had set foot on the island, chained with his brothers and sisters, his eyes had scanned the horizon of the white sandy beach. He looked towards the distant hills and mountain peaks lit up by the fading sunlight. This comforted him; all was not lost, and the plantation was not the only option for him. Quietly, and confidently, he had played the obedient and obliging African, carefully carrying out his chores. His master, astonished by his ability and manner, used him to make his plantation run more smoothly. Soon, Lumumba the old warrior organised and controlled the daily activities of many of this brothers and sisters in the cane piece. Now and again, the overseer raised his head to keep an eye on his charges, for he had more important things to do. He had to secure his own future, a small cane piece on or an animal pen maybe.

Unlike many of the African drivers, who were employed by the agents and overseers to ensure that their fellow Africans laboured uninterruptedly in the cane pieces, Lumumba began to prepare for the exit of his people. Using the careful and systematic actions, that had astonished and attracted his master;

he began plotting the pathways to the striking mountain peaks in the distance. The Africans dreamt of the peaceful hill and mountain valleys, away from the plantations as they toiled and slept. He knew this, so he prepared for this mass army waiting to flee.

They fled by themselves or in groups, sometimes directed by an 'insignificant spider', into the mountains that welcomed their new inhabitants; thus shielding them from the unrelenting demands of plantation slavery. In time, Lumumba fled from the plantation to the mountains with his extended family. They joined the shrinking bands of Taino people, as well as the early African Maroon communities there. They waged war on the planters. This lifted the hearts of the Africans and reinforced their determination to be free. It haunted, the sleeping and waking hours of the slave regimes.

One day, they were out hunting in their mountain refuge; suddenly, Lumumba stopped, as a bird squawked and flew into the air. Cautiously, they moved towards the place where the bird had left.

"Listen," he said, "these animals are our friends, they will tell us what is ahead if we study and trust them. Someone or something is ahead, take care," he warned.

"It is our countryman father, he is hurt. I can see blood on him, let's go to him quickly," the boy urged.

"He's a runaway, with the marks of a Yoruba tribesman and the branding of the Bax Hall plantation. He's been beaten, give me your water son," he insisted.

Lumumba moved towards his injured brother.

"Drink this, it will soothe your thirst. Cudjoe, go and tie some tree branches together to make a bed and a fan for our countryman," he directed urgently.

Returning with the entwined branches, Cudjoe doubled them and made a sleigh bed for the wounded runaway, and he fanned him vigorously. Moving him to the safety of the limestone cave they had just left, the injured man told them his story. A story they heard every day.

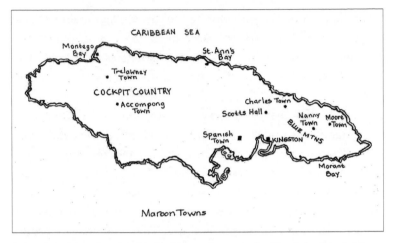

A drawing of Jamaica showing the Maroon towns and settlements. Adapted from: urbanintellectuals.com

"We wanted to join our brothers and sisters in the mountains. We arrived in a galleon from Goree Island a year ago. Some of us were bought by the Bax Hall Plantation. I was separated from my kinfolk, who sailed with me to the islands. They were purchased by the Bardiff Hall Plantation along the coast. We planned our escape because we knew that if we got to the mountains we would be free. We would also be able to help our folks, left on the plantations," he said gasping for breath.

"Soon after we left the cane piece, we were missed. They sent trackers and their dogs after us. For two days we managed to hide from them, we trudged through the streams and rivers in the dense forests and lost them, so they sent more dogs and men after us. We split up and hid as best as we could. They caught and beat me, then they hauled me down the side of a hill. I rolled over and kept plunging until I ended up here. I hid as best as I could. They thought I was dead, so they went after the others," he told them.

"You're too ill to travel, we'll rest in this cave. Cudjoe make use of the plants we found to help our brother. When you are better we will return to our compound together," he informed him.

Daily, they tended the wounded fugitives, that slowly swelled their armies of resistance against slavery. Like the first Maroons, Lumumba had created an alternative to plantation slavery. Noisily, they mourned their elder Lumumba when he had finished this important work and joined the ancestors' village, in their motherland. He was respected and honoured for his work, in recreating their ancestral home away from Africa. Later, his family members Cudjoe, Nanny, Accompong and Quao, became the leaders of the Maroons in the Eastern, Western and Southern mountains. Nanny and her fierce warriors defeated the British army, time and time again, becoming a thorn in their flesh. The British army destroyed their Great African Town.

The African runaways continued to build settlements within the island, in the rocky Cockpit country, as well as the mountain peaks, which extended across the island encircling it. Their paths to freedom were shortened, by links with the other ancient Taino and Maroon settlements; as well as the settlements led by the fierce warrior queen, Nanny in the East. Their settlements mushroomed across the island within the mountainous areas. They took on the communal living, of the continent, they had been snatched from. They shared the land and everything that was connected to it. They cared for the earth, the animals and the vegetation that gave them life and they also cared deeply for each other.

Every day, in the Maroon settlements in the mountains of the islands and the mainland, they waged war against the planters for their survival and continued liberty. Together, we would empty the plantations of many productive and valuable people, stolen from across our motherland. Our rebelliousness would ensure that the planters, would not rest comfortably in their beds at night and enjoy the gains from their enslavement, first of the Taino people and later the Africans. My brother and sisters had taken me across the ocean in their sub-consciousness, as well as within their hearts to comfort, support and inspire them to end their enslavement. I, Anancy, rose to the challenge.

CHAPTER 7

Nanny of the Maroons

Smoke spiralled into the lush and misty mountain peaks. The delicious smell of wild boars' meat, seasoned with pimento berries, miniature pointed multi-coloured peppers and cinnamon, filled their nostrils. The mouth-watering aroma revived them, after their exhausting trek across the rocky outcrops of the island; to the war council, at the Great African Town or Nanny Town in the East. Plantains, cassava, yams, peppers and maize stalks, simmer at the edges of the great fire, absorbing the meaty flavours. The pungent smell of rum laced with local berries, as well as the local brew stewed in calabash bowls and clay pots, fermented to quench their thirst. Our warrior Queen Nanny welcomed us.

"Welcome, elders." "Greetings from the women's and men's communities, respectively and all the settlements in the East. Pray, let us heartily welcome our elders from across the almost impassable mountain tracks of our island. We have among us elders from the Eastern parishes of Clarendon, Portland, St Andrew, St Catherine, St David, St Dorothy, and St Georges. Our family members have also come from St John, St Thomas in the East, St Thomas in the Vale and Vere. The Western parishes have sent us their elders too, they have come from Hanover, St Ann, St Mary, St James and Westmoreland of this magnificent island. They are weary, from their gruelling journey, across our hilly and mountainous isle. They bring us news of our family members in their compounds across the island, and this pleases us greatly," she told them jovially and lovingly.

Suddenly, her countenance changed, as she looked at the gathering solemnly.

"Our elders bring us good news, but also news we would rather not hear. Hear it we must, they bring news that the British government, the Council of Trade and Plantations and their army, intend to intensify their campaigns against us. They mean to drive us from our foothills and our mountaintop sanctuaries. These mountainous tracks that we were and are forced to live in and share was first occupied by the Taino people. Later, they became a place of safety and refuge for our ancestors when they were brought here by force. They left us this great town. It is a precious inheritance, which we cherish along with the freedom and dignity, it has given us as human beings."

A roar went around the gathering, as the words of their great warrior Queen Nanny, lifted their spirits and determination to confront the threat to their survival and continued freedom in the mountaintops.

"Let the British army, planters, the governor, the Council of Trade and Plantations and all the renegades they can muster come, we will be ready for them," the Maroons chanted.

The expressed sentiments drew them together, in their determination to defeat those who had tried to take their freedom. As well as the homes they had carved out of the precipitous mountainsides across the island, to be a free and dignified people. Reassured by the steely grit of the meeting, Nanny introduced me Anancy, to the gathering.

"You all know very well our brother, Anancy, the tireless defender of our freedom in our enforced home. He has brought a lot of information along with our scouts, of another impending attack on our settlement, by the British army so that we can be prepared. Let us show him how much we value his determined efforts, towards the freedom of those on the plantations as well as ourselves. We appreciate the immense comfort and assistance, he has given to all of us," she told them.

"Nightly, around our compound fires, we derive great comfort from the stories of our wise and often mischievous, brother Anancy. Temporarily, he eases our pain when we face dire confrontations with the slave masters, their overseers and drivers. The planters may have banned our mother tongues on their plantations, but they cannot take our Anancy stories from us, in our mountaintop shelters, or from our brothers and sisters in their cane pieces. Daily, we use these stories to talk to each other. We also use them to speak with our enslaved family members on their cane pieces, without their knowledge. The Backra can never comprehend the power of our Anancy stories, or wipe them from our consciousness. They are our strength and one of the weapons we use against them," she informed them.

My brothers and sisters cheered and applauded over and over again until my shiny black whiskers twitched and fluttered with love and embarrassment. Then, Nanny addressed us again, she continued with the pressing issue before us.

"As you already know, the flight of the Spanish settlers to Cuba and Hispaniola in 1655, after the British invasion, left vast tracts of fertile and flat land around the coast. The Council of Trade and Plantations initially had great difficulty persuading people from their country, with money to set up plantations. At that time, the situation worked in our favour. Our ancestors were able to live in the mountains and continue to use the foothills to farm their great plantain and yam walks. There were enough open spaces, for them to move between their settlements, in relative safety. We have inherited these mountain sanctuaries, we will cherish and look after this great town and pass it on to the next generation, to shield them from plantation slavery," she promised.

She paused and waited, as we echoed her wise words and demonstrated our aim and commitment, to preserving our freedom and inheritance, for future generations. She continued heartened by the steadfastness and fearlessness shown by everyone.

"Our great town nestles among these rocky openings; our provision grounds extend for miles at the foothills. We trade in the wild boar's meat within the island and across the seas; a trade the Taino people and our ancestors left us, and it has made us independent as well as given us some wealth. These uneven and craggy terrains, have kept us safe from the muskets and cannons, of the British army and Backra, up until now. We have been able to defeat all their attacks on us so far, because of the fighting skills and knowledge that have been passed down to us, from the elders."

Breathlessly, she carried on.

"The British army, the governor and the planters, fear attacks from their enemies to retake this island. The 1670 treaty, ceded this island to Great Britain; to stop attacks on Spanish galleons, by British pirates. They fear that we the Maroons across the island would support the Spanish government, army and former ranchers, waiting to take back this island. So from that point in time, they have tried to turn the lands around these foothills into plantations and fortresses to protect themselves. These new plantations encroach hugely on our farming and hunting grounds. Therefore, the conflict between us escalates minute by minute. They fear us because, as they steal more of our territory in the foothills, we continue to hunt and farm. We have shown them that we are not afraid, and we will not be controlled. We cannot withdraw because our survival depends on using the land around us. The land in these islands belongs to everyone. We are the guardians of these stony lands that we have been forced to live in, by the slave masters. The next generation will inherit them." she said defiantly.

We echoed her obstinacy, so she waited and then pick up where she had left off.

"Look, the Europeans have stolen the land that was created for all human beings and animals. They have sold it to men and women from their countries to the exclusion of all others. This is the insurmountable barrier that we face when dealing with the Backra and their notion of the ownership of the god given earth. How can someone steal the land, sell it for their own gain and then throw everyone off it and restrict their movements? They do not care, what happens to the people that have lived off, these vast tracts of land, for centuries before them. Then they try to force us, to work on their plantations without pay. They stubbornly refuse to accept, that all human beings have the right to be free, self-directing and be paid appropriately for their labour," she stated.

We shouted and cheered her on in the languages of our motherland.

"We should not only talk about the threat to us, but also the greater plight of our brothers and sisters on their plantations. Even though we live in the most inhospitable lands, we are free to live; we are privileged to be able to live in the ways of our fore-parents in Africa. Yet, our relatives are worked to death, beaten and mutilated every day of their lives. Slavery has taken away their freedom and human dignity; they barely exist as human beings. We are our brothers and sisters' keeper. We must, therefore, fight one battle, for our continued freedom and their liberation from the plantations. We gladly accept them into our community, when they come to us as the Taino people did for us, in the past. However, this is not enough, in the future we must work towards the total freedom of every enslaved person. Slavery is an abomination to humanity," she told them.

Reinvigorated by her wise words, we were energised to confront the task ahead; yet again and our voices showed this. Then she continued.

"As long as our brothers and sisters, on the plantations are forced to work without pay, we are not free, we cannot be free. The plight of those on the plantations and ours are the same. Every time, the Backra look at those that they have enslaved, they remind them of us and the free labour they could have if we were in their cane pieces. They would feel secure because there would be no-one to challenge them if we were back on their plantations and give those in their midst the hope of freedom. They are infuriated because we assert our rights as equal human beings. They accuse us of trespassing on their land, land which contains wild animals, crops and trees that belong to no-one but the gods, the spirits and the forces of nature. When they steal our people and force them into slavery, we raid the plantations and take them back. We unite families that the slave masters have callously separated and sold throughout the islands and the mainland. Our actions are just and humane; we abhor the coldness and money grabbing ways, of the Backra and their government. These are the reasons we must stand steadfastly, against their aggression and inhumanity. However, they fear us most of all because they have never been able to defeat us, in the constant wars they have waged against us, to enslave us in the past," she pointed out.

A jubilant cry went up from the assembled elders, weary and almost out of breath after her long and inspirational welcome, she took her seat among us. We repeated the sentiments of our warrior Queen Nanny, to strengthen ourselves for the inevitable battles ahead.

"We will never return to the plantations, our ancestors were not enslaved. The Akan, Ibo, Mandingo, Coromanti and Yoruba peoples, who arrived on the Spanish galleons from Spain, fled to the mountains. The majority of the mountain people were born on these mountaintops, and they are free Africans. We will never be enslaved, however much they enclose our land and settle soldiers in the foothills and make military fortresses around our settlements," we declared stubbornly.

The sun travelled across the sky, it indicated dusk and nightfall. The elders eager to meet family members left the compound without delay. They headed for the villages perched on the mountaintops, almost touching the sky. They exchanged happy and sad events, as families and friends do in the Great African Town. Later, they returned to the warrior queen's compound to celebrate and enjoy the huge feast that had been prepared for them. The drums beat quietly and harmoniously, in the language and spirit of their ancestors. They danced and sang in their mother tongues, dressed in the costumes of their motherland, led by the colourful Junkanoo masquerades and processions.

The Maroons in the mountains almost touching the sky did not fear the British. They feared losing their freedom and dignity, as human beings and Africans. The British army and the government knew this and so they sought to remove these spikes in their flesh. The Maroons and runaways in the rocky regions of the island prevented them from feeling secure and in total control of their islands and their plantations within them.

Their aim and dream were to rid the island of the Great African Town in the East, which stood as a symbol of the Maroons' rebelliousness, freedom and enormous strength. The mountain-dwelling Maroons had defeated the planters' armies time and time again, over the years. Their pride was severely wounded. However, it was the astronomical amounts of money, to be made from growing sugar, as well as the prestige and power it bestowed on them, which dictated their actions against them.

The second day of the elders' visit to the mountains that almost touched the sky, was a practical one. Nanny greeted her extended family with a hearty breakfast, of the delight, that could only be found in these mountainous kingdoms. Next, we gave our gifts. We had brought spears, weapons and vital intelligence to defend our ancestral home, in the East. We also donated muskets, gunpowder and smaller equipment captured from the British army or bought from the pirates, buccaneers, Jewish-Portuguese merchants on the island. We brought weapons that had been smuggled into the island, by Africans from the Spanish and French speaking islands and the mainland. We gave everything we could, to defend the Great African Town in the East. The survival of the Great African Town in the East ensured that the Maroons would continue to live in freedom. Our biggest gift was our determination to defeat slavery whatever the cost.

After lengthy goodbyes, we returned to our various mountainous communities across the island while our Great African Town in the East, prepared for the assault of the British army and planters yet again.

CHAPTER 8

The campaign

The British government and the planters worked vigorously to secure their newly acquired colonies. They had to protect them, from both the internal threat posed by the enslaved Africans and the Maroons in the mountaintops, as well as the external one represented by the monarchies of Europe.

Continuously, I worked with my brothers and sisters in the mountains and with the enslaved Africans on the plantations; together we escalated our war against the planters. We would destroy slavery and so we faced the slave masters and their armies squarely on the battlefield, in the mountainous country, on the plantations and in their lofty meeting places. Collectively, we engaged the Backra and their allies, with as much force as we could muster.

Incessantly, the planters fumed, raged and moaned. They whined about the ingratitude and reluctance of their Blackies to cheerfully and industriously work from sunrise to sunset, to grow sugar to enrich them. I secreted myself in their meeting places, high in the rafters. I took the Backras' pre-occupation with them to the mountains, thus reducing some of the heavy blows and injuries that would be inflicted on them. I revealed their detailed plans to crush their resistance.

"We bring them here", the planters wailed, "at enormous cost to ourselves. The minute they are landed on the beaches or very soon after, the ungrateful brutes sprint to the mountains to join that godless Negress, Nanny. We lose hours and hours of their labour, as well as the time and the money we spend on returning them to our cane pieces. The government and this council begged us to come and set up plantations. We have risked our money and our lives to do so and what is the result? Daily, there are attacks on our plantations, as well as slaves who run to the fugitives in the mountains, the minute the overseers and drivers' backs are turned. I have lost money; it is touch and go if my plantation in the East lasts until the next planting season," moaned a dreary and tired looking planter.

Next, the planters' representative addressed the assembly.

"The plantation owners in the East, have tried in vain to run their estates efficiently, on the land the King sold to us, at excessive prices. Our efforts have come to nothing so far. Fearlessly, the Maroon bands strut across our plantations, to take the animals and crops, which they apparently grew and hunted there in the past. We have not been able to stop them. They regard the land that we now 'own' as open to all those who live there now and in the past. The local militiamen in the East, are no match for them," he said.

"They are skilful at moving about. We have been forced to abandon our plantations for the time being until the Maroon question is settled. Daily, our slaves run away to the mountains to join our greatest foe, that immoral Negress, who directs the war against us. Naturally, they prefer the mountains, where they can work for themselves and their families in freedom. The exodus must be stopped, or else the East will be controlled from the mountains by that godless Negress," the representative warned.

"The survival of all our plantations on this island is in grave danger if the island is recaptured by the Spanish," added a troubled planter.

"I personally, have seen the movement of goods and weapons from the coast, across the lowlands to the highlands, under the cover of darkness. The recapture of this island is being planned, mark my words. The Spanish messengers meet the Maroon leaders, in the coves and inlets along the coast at night; you can imagine their trade, trade in muskets and gunpowder. We have slaves on our plantations, who by magic or by other means, move between our plantations, the islands and the mainland. The sooner we remove the Maroons from the mountaintops and onto our plantations, the better it will be for us," advised the representative.

"The Maroons in the mountains and the Spanish, have common cause to drive us from this island because they were here before us. The Spanish are plotting right now, to take back their island with the help of the Maroons and anyone who will help them," wailed another planter.

"Pray tell us what the army and the governor, are doing about this diabolical situation," they insisted.

Violently, my limbs shook at their bleating and grumbling. They attacked my family members for not obediently and conscientiously growing sugar on their plantations while castigating the Maroons for hunting in the foothills to feed themselves and their communities. Uncontrollably, I seethed and fumed with rage, as they complained and moaned. I struggled to restrain myself without success.

As they flung their questions and demands, at the officials, the governor and the general, I added a couple of my own. In a high pitched and chilling voice, in the manner of those who by magic or by other means move between the islands, the mainland and their plantations. I asked the Backra, why they had not paid the enslaved Africans on their plantations for their work? Surely, I told them in my most spooky and piercing voice, that their slaves would work harder if they lived and worked in freedom. My voice boomed and bounced off the four walls of their meeting room.

They reacted as I had expected. The Backra looked around the room for the intruder, rage and fear engulfed them; while their hair pieces flew off and their receding hair stood on end. The colour of their faces moved along a continuum from strawberry red to a deathly blue tinge. Wildly, they trembled and shivered. Pandemonium filled the room; they huddled together to protect themselves and each other. However, they jumped apart as they touched, fearing the malicious forces within their midst.

"Who would make such a spiteful suggestion?" they bleated together.

Their voices squeaked and trembled dreadfully.

"It cannot be one of us because we are of one mind in this venture. It must be a Spanish, Dutch or French spy among us making these ghastly and unholy suggestions."

They spun around and scrutinised each other, to locate the dissenting trespasser.

"How can we make money and also pay our slaves; these two ideas are incompatible? Slavery makes us wealthy and gives us the power to exert over our slaves," they mumbled crossly.

"If we paid them, then our income would diminish. We would not be able to maintain our lavish and comfortable lifestyles, on our estates and in our stately homes in England," groaned a planter.

"I bet", said another planter trembling, "it is the Obeah people on our plantations. They dare to come among us and make these offensive suggestions. Only they would want our slaves to be paid and that's why we cannot see them. They are trying to work their magic on us. We must purge our plantations, of the Obeah men and women who hide among our slaves and incite them to do us great mischief. They have used us ill; daily they ferment rebellions on our plantations. They kill the children we breed, with our slave women to work in our great houses. We must rid our plantations, of these evil and deceitful Blackies," they declared.

"We must find ways to replace their magic with our magic. We must return our plantations to peace, productivity and profit," they mumbled aggressively.

I was tempted to spin, a gigantic knotty web around the assembled infidels and squeeze every ounce of breath from, their gluttonous and gorged bodies. I decided against it, as it would give away our secrets and our strengths. Fearfully, they left for their plantations, to root out the malicious forces that threatened their future. In the distant past, they had dismissed the Obeah men and women of their slaves, as figments of their infantile state. As the years passed, they were forced to acknowledge the power of these Negroes, on their plantations. They would make them pay, for entering their meeting place, with their lives.

The following week, the planters and their representatives again met with the general and his officers, they requested prompt action against the rebels in the mountaintops. The general went on the offensive; he hoped to deflect some of their criticisms.

"The British army and its officers, have not been sitting idly by while our slaves and the Maroons have been running amuck on this island and all our other islands," he assured them.

"Our campaigns against the Maroon communities and the runaway slaves in the mountains and especially in the East, have been constant and meticulous," he stressed scathingly.

He continued in the most vexed and exhausting tone.

"You must understand what we are up against. The mountainous landscape of the island impedes our fight against the Maroon bands. These fugitives are now scattered across the island at this point in time. As you all know, attacks on plantations in the East have always been a major problem. The ridges and inclines of the mountainous landscape have been the stronghold of the Maroon bands from the time of the Spanish; they are well established and well defended. We have failed time and time again, to dislodge the Maroons in the Great African Town in the East. Time and time again, we have lost to their expert armies, due to the leadership of their warrior queen," he told them.

"The records show the victories of the Maroons, over our military again and again. However, we will not give up, we will find a way into their mountainous stronghold to weaken and destroy them," he informed them.

Then he introduced them to a Colonel, who had recently arrived on the island. He had fought many campaigns in the Eastern countries, where he was successful in evicting rebellious savages, lodged in mountainous enclaves.

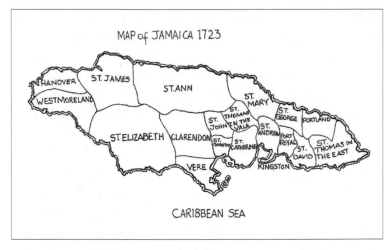

Parish divisions of the island of Jamaica 1723. Adapted from caribbeanexams.com

He introduced the Colonel to the assembled planters. He addressed them solemnly.

"I understand your anger sirs, to be challenged, and your livelihoods disrupted by these savages is intolerable. I will put a stop to this unheard of situation, with the help from you all," the Colonel told them.

"I have heard of the skill of the barbarians in the mountaintops, but I assure you, they will be put in their place. Those animals can and will be tamed. I have been in the Eastern colonies where I had to tame a group of beasts who would not submit to the rule of the King of England. It took many attempts, but we routed them in one of the most perilous peaks in that country and I will do it again," he promised them.

"I must admit, we lack well-trained fighting soldiers and equipment and this has weakened our campaigns against the barbarians in the past. We must use their own tactics of hit and run, to destroy and return them to the plantations. This will help those of you, who are trying to establish plantations in the East. The defeat of these brutes will also stop the flight of your slaves, to the mountains too," he assured them.

The planters' countenances perked up. They offered their services to this Colonel, who promised them a future with obedient slaves on their plantations and mountains without ferocious Maroons. He guaranteed the Maroons' demise. He told them about the machinery, he had used in the Eastern colonies against the savages.

"These weapons will have to be ordered and probably made by gunsmiths in England. These new weapons are efficient and destructive; they will end the Negro dominance in the East. However, it will take a year or two before we can get them to the island. In the meantime, we will find other ways of taking the war to those brutes in the mountains. There are many drifting souls, rudderless soldiers and private armies out there, to be recruited to fight for us if the rewards are high enough. We will offer them good rates of pay and land in the foothills to grow sugar when they drive the Maroons armies from the mountains. Then, you will have an instant supply of Negroes, to produce sugar. We must give them the best training we can; these desperate souls fear no-one or nothing. They will bring the savages to heel," I assure you.

"We will use the rainy season, to train these would be soldiers, find equipment and plot our routes, into the mountaintops. At the end of the rainy season, we will drive them from their Great African Town and destroy it," he vowed.

The planters hollered and cheered, it was the first time in years that they felt that, the situation could be turned in their favour. They left the meeting, each and everyone determined to help this brave Colonel, defeat the savages, in their mountain fortresses. In the interim, the Colonel assembled his ragged and desperate army. He trained them in the use of muskets and gunpowder. The Colonel put his men, into two battalions of a hundred fighting men, as well as their scouts and baggage handlers. He trained a dozen scouts to watch and bring back information from the mountain, about the routine of the Maroons. Next, he sent out a small party to gather information on and map the secret routes into the Great African Town. They recruited Maroons and enslaved Africans, who gave them this information, the position of their most significant settlement and their plans to defend it.

The planters were generous to the Colonel and his army. They gave food, animals, equipment, money and many of their slaves, to fight the Maroons in the East. At the beginning of the dry season, the soldiers led by their Colonel took the path to the mountainous slopes. They climbed and climbed, without any challenge from the Maroons. The Colonel's confidence soared, as they came nearer and nearer to the Great African Town, by an unknown route without being challenged. He ordered the two divisions, to enter the town from different sides of the mountain, to out-manoeuvre the Maroons fighters when they were discovered. They camped for the night. They would come together as the sun rose, to attack the Great African Town.

The Maroon armies had not expected, the British army's climb up the mountainside, by the route known only to myself, the fighters and the elders. Indeed, this Colonel was very determined. Briefly, they had been out-manoeuvred by the Colonel and his army. Strenuously, they chided themselves for their great mistake, that could have ended the freedom of the mountain community and make the island one big sugar plantation. Quickly, the information was passed to our warrior chief Nanny and the assembled fighters, who acted immediately as well as decisively.

As the first battalion slept, the Maroon army attacked their camp. They woke in disarray. They ran down the vertical mountainsides and tumbled over the solid cliff faces and ledges, on a very dark night. Hidden in the openings in the mountainsides, the Maroon fighters shoved the disorientated soldiers, over the rock-hard inclines. Then, they surrounded the sleeping battalion, on the other side of the mountain and waited.

As the sun rose, the eager Colonel assembled his army recruits for the battle, unaware of the events during the night, on the other side of the mountain ridge. The Colonel ordered his men to hold their ground, as the other battalion would join them very soon. Together, they would enter the town and take it.

The Maroon armies took up their positions, between the windswept cliff faces camouflaged with branches, plants and boulders. They waited until the soldiers were in their most exposed location. They fired on them, using the guns and ammunition they had taken from the first battalion during the night. Unable to see them, the soldiers fired into the air; soon their ammunition was exhausted. They flew down the precipitous mountainsides. They fell over cliffs and gullies, into steaming and raging water holes.

The zealous Colonel rushed to the other side of the mountain, with his remaining men to join the other division. On their way, they met a few of the surviving soldiers from the first group, they told him about the ambush in the night. The Colonel agreed to abandon the campaign when he learnt of the amount of ammunition that was taken from them. He assured the surviving men, they would be back. It was only a temporary setback. They had been overwhelmed, but with the knowledge of the mountain routes and the new and efficient weaponry, they would be successful next time.

In the meantime, led by our warrior Queen Nanny, we planned for the next attack. For the time being, life in the mountains returned to normal. The Maroons hunted the wild boar; they planted on lands in the foothills, which crossed newly acquired plantations. They re-organised their settlements in the mountains. They cleared the extensive forests around them to grow food, to meet their restructured community.

As usual, the deflated planters and the surviving soldiers drank rum to raise their spirits in defeat. They were infuriated that the Colonel's swagger and promise had not materialised. They told themselves that when the new and efficient weapons arrived, the Maroons would be defeated and they would have more of their free labour for their plantations. They waited for that day. Meticulously, we all prepared for that day too.

CHAPTER 9

Intuition

Nanny walked through the bright green ferns, that rustled against her firm black calves. She ambled along the well-trodden pathways, that looked down on the Great African Town, this impressive town named in her honour. Instinctively, she moved through the dense vegetation, towards a clearing. It gave her a panoramic view, of the Maroon compounds nestled in the valleys, between the wind-swept mountain slopes. For a minute, she was in awe of the genius of the Taino people and her ancestors. They had carved out a livelihood and refuge in these perilous slopes and the bottomless abyss away from the Spanish, and then the British invaders, over two hundred years before.

Tears trickled down her cheeks, bronzed by the hot sun overhead, as she remembered the brave warriors that had died, defending these scanty and sparse lands. The British planters and their army begrudged them these harsh and marginal terrains. So, they had continually tried to evict them. They sought to return them to their plantations and steal and own every inch of land, even if they could not use it. She reflected on their most recent encounter, with the British army and its renegade bands. They had climbed the solid and slippery mountainsides by the back route, to return her and her people to their plantations. She brooded on the next unavoidable encounter, with the planters and their armies, it preoccupied her.

She brushed these thoughts aside, as she tried to enjoy the solitude and peace of the stunning mountain scenery around her, for a few hours. She mused on the fact, that her army had outmanoeuvred them, yet again. They had forced the red and white-clad soldiers and their allies down the mountainsides in humiliation and to their deaths. The cocksure young Colonel had promised the planters, the Negro warrior queen and the Great African Town in the mountain, but he had failed yet again. He would be back to restore his tattered reputation; a shudder ran down her spine, and this troubled her terribly.

In all her years as a leader of the Maroons, she had never felt so threatened by any of the British officers, that had forced their way up the almost impenetrable mountainsides. This Colonel intended to return them to the plantations and destroy their Great African Town and plantain-walks. This arrogant young Colonel had come close to their principal dwelling-place, by the unknown route. It was a warning they had to heed. She looked up to the heavens and asked her great ancestors, the gods, the wind, the sun and rain that sustained these dense magnificent mountain cliffs to guide her. They had to find the right strategies, to continue to defend their great civilisations and freedom in the mountains.

Nanny turned quickly, she looked behind her as a twig broke, shattering her reverie. The noise forced her back to the cool and calm, of the sheer and sloping pathways that she dearly loved. A huge Guango tree spread its shading branches across the vast expanse. An enormous branch shaded her from the scorching sun. She noticed on a branch close to her, a giant spider's web. The arachnid was twirling its body around and around as if building its home. Her eyes were drawn to the strong, robust threads, which glowed, quivered and shimmered in the sun. She peered at it, as the spider's body made the most elaborate movements. It was unlike anything she had seen before; she moved closer to observe.

The swift movements of the spider amused her. She wondered if this was her brother Anancy's way of informing her without intruding on her self-imposed isolation of future events to come. She smiled at his thoughtfulness and resourcefulness. Intently, she looked at the web. In the shimmering threads, she imagined that she saw, the scowling face of the British Colonel. Agitatedly, he walked to and fro in his makeshift tent that was

Jamaican National Heroine, Nanny of the Maroons, drawn from the official 1976 portrait.

now his home and army camp against the inhabitants in the mountaintops. Nanny thought she recognised, a look of steadfast purpose and determination on his face. The same unwavering determination, that she and the Maroons clung to in the mountains, to maintain their human dignity and freedom, denied to them by plantation slavery. In his singled-minded features and posture, she felt an omen for the future. She saw or thought she saw, glimpses of the metals he sketched and drew. He was designing a contraption, to end the Maroons' defiance of the planters and their government.

She reflected on the genius, of the hit and run strategies that she and her army had developed and used, in the vertical cliff tops. They had used them to wage war on and defeat the military and the planters again and again. She wondered about the new instruments of war, represented by this brash Colonel. They would have to revise their strategies, in the face of what she had seen, as the new threat in the spider's web. Over the centuries, the Taino people and her ancestors had had to adapt and rethink their strategies. They had to fine-tune them, to meet the relentless attacks on them, first by the Spanish and then by the British invaders. Once again, the survival of the community in the mountaintops had to be her priority. Every insight, every premonition and intelligence had to be scrutinised painstakingly, to preserve their freedom and dwelling place.

For a moment, she trembled and shivered. Then, she became aware of her feelings of fear and helplessness. She composed herself and looked steadily at the vast ridges and emerald mountainsides. They had given them and their predecessors, centuries of human dignity and control over their lives, away from the plantations. Her people had been forced into these perilous, but stunning mountain cliff tops to live in freedom, to live and share the abundant lands, which nature had provided for all the inhabitants of the earth. They had refashioned these once inhospitable terrains, to accommodate and protect them. These lands had no preference, for any particular group of people, whatever their colour. Yet, the slave masters and their accomplices begrudged them of these harsh terrains because they had chosen to retreat into them. They had refused to give them their labour. Instead, they would use it collectively to benefit themselves and their community.

The Backra could not forgive, the Taino people and later the Maroons, for withdrawing their labour and person from them.

Nanny pondered her people's future, as she descended the plunging mountain slopes to the elders, warriors and community. She had to plan for the inevitable assault from the planter's army to dislodge and enslave them forever. Nanny thanked me, through the winds and forces of nature that surrounded her, for warning her of the British army and planters', plans to destroy their mountain sanctuary.

The preparations for the forthcoming war gathered a feverish pitch. The Great African Town had to be restructured once again, to withstand whatever the barefaced Colonel and his army had in store for them. He would aim to take the town by whatever means, this would restore his and the British army's battered reputation.

Swiftly, Nanny and the elder council agreed to decentralise their ancient settlement. Immediately, new lands were cleared, within the wild and the unruly terrain on the mountainsides and families were allocated to them. Their valuables and wealth were hidden insides these new settlements. Life continued in the great town, the battle for their sanctuary and refuge, preoccupied their waking and sleeping hours. In the new satellite compounds, the families and their animals worked, played and lived.

Meanwhile, in the remote and ancient Maroon settlements across the North, South and West of the island, the elders prepared to welcome their brothers and sisters, from the Great African Town if necessary. Nanny and the elders had used their meeting to review and make contingency plans, for the big assault, from the upstart of a Colonel and his army.

At the end of the rainy season, the Maroon scouts and I brought the expected news, of the stirring of the British army. Their ships were offshore, and they were laden with tonnes of metal pieces in metal boxes, which would be stored in their camps and forts. The Maroon scouts and I skirted the forts to gain vital information, but the heavily guarded forts held their secrets. The sealed boxes would not entertain even the smallest spider. We knew about the new-fangled weaponry that the British army had used elsewhere against the Spanish and French armies as well as others with great success. So the Maroon army, prepared the ledges leading up to the vertical mountainsides, to disrupt and hinder the progress, of whatever the Army had in store for them.

The Maroon armies waited and waited for the attack, but it did not come. Their preparation had halted the progress, of the British soldiers who had tried to scale the dense mountainsides, with their new and heavy weapons. They returned to their forts, to fix and ponder how to get their massive armoury, closer to and within the range of the Great African Town. They re-grouped in their forts and repaired their huge swivel cannons. They had to revise their strategy, so they took their time over it. In the meantime, the Maroon scouts and I planned and carried out, much-needed surveillance to be prepared.

After some months, our scouting bore fruit. We were warned of the advance of the British soldiers and their single-minded Colonel. Their dismantled weapons were enclosed in fortified forts, hastily thrown up around the outskirts of our town. They were guarded day and night, by many armed soldiers. Again, the Maroon armies waited for the attack, but again the army withdrew and were silent.

Once again the Maroon army descended the weather-beaten mountainsides. They reinforced the massive boulders along the rocky projections and sides of the pathways into the mountains, to stop the army's weaponry from leaving their hastily constructed forts. They dug deep into the landscape, to enlarge openings in the undulating land, to block the entry of their heavy weapons. Again, I tried to enter their fortified forts and the vast metal boxes contained within. But again, the boxes held their secrets. So the Maroon armies built up their defences, in the thick foliage that shielded them from, the glare of the sun and their enemies.

All of a sudden, one morning at the crack of dawn, the attack on the Great African Town began. The long metal parts, of the swivel weapons above the town, belched and threw out tonnes of raging fire and dust, on the settlement across the valley. Smoke and dust choked everyone and blinded their eyes. The Maroon army responded with their muskets and gunpowder. However, they were forced to retreat as the glowing dust and balls of fire flew around them, threatening to scorch them. Across another ridge, a moving cannon spurted smouldering cast-iron balls, that flattened some houses, as well as the semi-dry woodlands around them.

The British soldiers and their weapons were out of reach. The sly young Colonel had abandoned armed combat, in favour of the moving armaments with extended metal limbs. These were spun in all directions swiftly, to scatter the Maroons armies and keep them at bay.

The Maroon armies spread out, into the land around their town, to wait for a lull in the bombardment. Then they would move to the older established settlements in the North, South and West of the island. They would rebuild their new town, in the mountains around the Great African Town in the future. The elders assembled and discussed the destruction of their ancient dwelling place. They vowed that their principal settlements would no longer be within the reach of the British army, especially with their moving weapons with limbs. The fighters revised their military strategies, in the light of the British army's new weaponry and their flattened great town, now in the hands of the British army.

CHAPTER 10

The Maroons are scattered

The officials of the Council of trade and plantations, the governor and the army general gathered for a riotous celebration. Finally, they had dispersed the Maroon armies and flattened their great town, in the East. Fortunately, for the Maroons, they did not have any of their body parts to put on spikes, to parade around their capital in Spanish Town. The planters could not show the public, what they considered their 'great victory' over the Maroons in the East at last. This was the first time the British army, had left the precipitous mountains in triumph and their bodies, intact because they had avoided close fighting with the Maroon warriors. Now, they dreamt of even more great victories, against those brazen Africans, who had withheld their labour from their plantations and dared to challenge them.

The Backra was keen to revive their fortunes. Now, they could expand their cane pieces in the East. Their earnings would grow threefold, without the constant threat from the Maroons bands in search of animals and food from the land around their plantations. The Maroons in the East began to rebuild their settlements. They waited for the chance to rebuild their Great African Town once again.

The majority of the Maroons had chosen new leaders and had trekked towards the South, West and North of the island. They were enthusiastically welcomed by their family members in the ancient Maroon settlements, concealed in the mountain chains across the Southern, Northern and Western parishes. Their numbers swelled these communities. These enlarged settlements had to feed their growing population from the East. They also

A building from the time of the Spanish, St Jago de la Vega, Spanish capital of Jamaica from 1534.

had to provide for the increased numbers of enslaved people, who took the opportunity to join them, as they watched them move across the island.

The Backra, the Council and the army, strutted about in their newly found confidence. They were very slow to realise that the attack on the Great African Town had unlocked, the age-old problem of the freedom and ownership of the magnificent peaks, sloping and flat landscapes, of the island. The enlarged settlements across the island had to hunt and farm in the foothills on the lands around their plantations. They had to feed their increased numbers. Naturally, they used all the land, which nature had provided for all the inhabitants of the earth, at no cost.

As the Maroons hunted for wild boar and other animals to feed their families, trade and plant their great plantain-walks, they crossed the vast tracts of fertile land that the planters had stolen from the Taino people. They now owned all the land, because they had paid a small sum of money to enclose it. Ruthlessly, they had exploited their free labour in the gold and silver mines, pearl fisheries and much later in their sugar and coffee plantations.

However, very soon their jubilation ceased. Angry and frustrated, the planters in the West and North of the island crowded together. They objected to the growing bands of Maroons in their midst and the increased flight of their slaves to the mountaintops. They protested about the now frequent insurrections, on their plantations, as these disrupted their smooth running. These insurgencies threatened their families, employees and themselves. Many of the cowardly Backra left their estates in the hands of their agents and overseers. They retired to their stately homes in England. The majority of the plantations on the island were now owned by absentee planters.

The remaining slave owners and their representative protested to their Parliament, the governor, the council and the general about the new threat they now faced, from the enlarged Maroon settlements on the island. They blamed the army and especially the bold young Colonel, who had bombarded the great town in the East. He had dispersed the Maroon bands, across the island to their once quiet and flourishing sugar plantations. They demanded action to stop, the enlarged groups of Maroons, hunting on their land. They stressed that they would happily deal with the Maroon bands, but they did not have the experience, the guns, militia or confidence to challenge the outlaws, individually or collectively. So they begged and nagged the governor and the army to remove the increased threat to their livelihoods, in the West from the Maroons.

Deep in the harsh landscape of the island, the Maroon bands and their new leaders, also contemplated their new situation. The destruction of Nanny Town had been a tremendous blow and shock to them, as well as the enslaved Africans across the island. The Maroon settlements had only known, total victory over the planters and their armies, for more than two hundred years. They had kept the Backra and their armies, from their marginal lands, in their ancient settlements. Now in these antiquated dwelling places of their ancestors, they would have to ensure that they remained many steps ahead of the planters and their armies. They would have to make sure that their principal settlements were out of the reach of the British army's new weaponry.

Carefully, they chose the most inaccessible mountaintops, to build their new communities. They revitalised their existing ones, hidden in the recesses of the mountain chains in the South, West and Northwestern parishes of the island. In the future, their settlements would be out of the reach of the British army's big swivel guns, with their extended metal limbs.

CHAPTER 11

The Maroons are under pressure yet again

The planters congregated in the governor's office, in the elegant red brick building in Spanish Town once again. The planters' representatives came from the parishes in the West and North of the island, where the ancient Maroon settlements had been enlarged, by the migration from Nanny Town in the East.

For the umpteenth time, they wrung their hands. They moaned about the disorder, that had wrecked their former tranquil and peaceful existence, on their plantations with their agreeable slaves. Again, they castigated and cursed the actions of the rash young Colonel, who had attacked their great town and scattered its cantankerous inhabitants. They talked about the great evils, that now disrupted their everyday lives. Daily, these substantial hordes crossed their plantations, to hunt wild animals or take their livestock. They moaned that when their militias tried to stop them entering their plantations; they took their guns and the wild animals they had been hunting and returned to the mountains.

However, they complained bitterly about the effect it had on their slave populations. The actions of the Maroon bands seriously encouraged their slaves to openly defy them. They threatened to join the Maroons in the mountains if their demands were not met. They moaned that after giving into many of them, the slaves joined the Maroons in the mountains anyway.

The bombardment by the young Colonel, of the African town in the East, had disrupted and reduced sugar production on their plantations. They pleaded for action against what they called 'the savage Maroon bands' that now roamed the entire island. They warned, that if the governor and the army did not do something very soon, they would have to give up their plantations and seek their fortune elsewhere. Their rivals could have this money-making sugar island. They warned that the Maroons were so powerful now, that they were spread across the length and breadth of the island in huge numbers, they could drive them off the island if they wanted to.

The slave owners warned about the leader of the Great African Town, Nanny, once again, they stressed that although her town was bombarded years before, she still had great influence over the Maroon communities within the island. The destruction of their township had given her the opportunity to strategically fling, her Maroon brigands across the island. Now, she was unofficially in control of their island. On a daily basis, her scouts crossed the seas to Cuba and St Domingue to trade, but they also knew she was plotting with the Spaniards, to take back the island. They were convinced that the Spanish government had a plan to give the Maroons their own lands, on the island and sign a peace treaty with them. If this came to pass, they warned, the devilish Negro woman would free all their slaves. The slaves would drive them and the British administration into the sea. This could not be allowed to happen.

They recounted horrific stories, of the Negro woman's witchcraft. This vindictive hag had caused British soldiers to jump from high cliffs and ledges flying as if they were birds. It was widely known, that she had boiled British soldiers in her huge cauldron, in the mountains. They concluded that the bombardment of their town in the East had been a ghastly error. It had flung the Maroons, across the island in huge numbers, to torment and disrupt their once peaceful plantations. The result was that sugar production and their incomes had plummeted. The slave masters pleaded for something to be done, to allow them to do what they had come to the island to do. They were there to grow sugar and make a lot of money for themselves, the King of England and their country.

The army general answered them in the most scathing manner. He stressed their unexpected destruction of the African town five years before. He also listed the many campaigns they had lost against the Maroons, led by their warrior queen, Nanny. He assured them that the army had not been idly sitting around while the Maroons raided their plantations and carried off their slaves and goods. Time and time again, he told them, the army had gone after them in their settlements in the West. He reminded them that it was the resolute assault on the Maroon Town that had propelled and entrenched them across the island in reinforced settlements, which the army had little hope of getting close to or destroying.

He told them, it would be more difficult now, for the military to defeat them because they had learnt from the destruction of their town in the East. They had built their townships deep into the mountain interior, with one entrance and many exits. The British army would not try to enter those bottomless limestone caves and mountain precipices. It would be reckless. He informed them that they would have to find new ways of encouraging the Maroons to work with them, as this, he had concluded, was the only way forward.

They had lost all their campaigns against them, except for the bombardment of their town in the East. The town had already been abandoned by its inhabitants and its leaders. More military campaigns against them were not the answer to the problems facing them.

I listened to the wretched planters, who had stolen the vast and productive lands of the Taino people and then they had enslaved and very nearly exterminated them. The remainder had fled to the mountains, leaving them with their rich and fertile coastal lands. The British invaders had replaced the Spanish. They were now using the free labour of the Africans, to amass enormous incomes from growing sugarcane. They had used their ill-gotten wealth, to build grand estates and country houses, elegant churches and civic buildings, in their countries of origin. The incomes from the labour of the enslaved Africans, in their cane pieces, had ensured the British dominance of the oceans, trade, insurance and the finances of the world. Yet, they

An original section of a wall of a fort built to house slaves before they were shipped to the Spanish, French and British colonies by British slave traders in Jamaica.

continued to whine about my brothers and sisters in the mountains, defending their negligible freedoms, as well as the enslaved Africans on their plantations, which they and their drivers and overseers brutalised from dawn to dusk, to create wealth for themselves.

My patience had run out, I would terrorise and place a wedge between them. I intervened in their meeting again and spoke on behalf of my enslaved brothers and sisters. I used the general's voice to put forward their grievances. He spoke with passion, to the assembled planters and their representative.

"The Maroons are fighting principally to retain their freedom, naturally they want to live in the ways of their family members and ancestors in Africa," he told them.

Then he continued.

"The enslaved Africans on your plantations are human beings. They have the right to be free and be paid for their labour. The Maroons, as well as the Africans in your cane pieces, are an inventive and intelligent people. Look how the Maroons effortlessly strut, across the hilly and mountainous landscape of this island and your plantations. Their skilful mastery of the rugged environment has kept our armies at bay. They have defeated us time and time again in battle and they will continue to do so in the future," he told them haughtily.

"We have used our white skins to justify the enslavement of the Taino people and now the Africans by claiming to be superior human beings. Dangerously, we deceive ourselves that they are somehow 'lesser than us'. It is our love of money and our craving for more and more of it that have dictated our cold-blooded actions towards these gentle and cultured peoples," he informed them.

"Deep in our hearts we know that we are the uncivilised brutes, because of our enslavement and ruthless treatment of these noble and generous peoples. We have no right to call ourselves human beings. Our white skins are profoundly polluted with our horrendous crimes against the Taino, the Africans and humanity. This will always be the case, no matter how many reasons we find to defend our atrocious behaviour and actions," he pointed out to them.

Again, the Backras' wigs bobbed up and down on their pulsating skulls. Their faces turned to many shades of crimson with rage, at the words that came from the general's lips.

"The weather has got the better of him, he has gone mad," they bleated.

"He speaks for the Blackies on our plantations and the savages in the mountaintops," they hollered and shrieked.

The gathering pounced on him and knocked him to the floor; he fell with a loud and deafening thud, he appeared stiff and dazed. They stood aloof from him, with scorn and contempt on their puffed and scarlet faces. The planters peered at the man who looked like them but now spoke as the champion of their slaves. They turned him over and over with their feet. However, he remained in a stiff and trance-like state. In a panic, they grabbed a bottle of rum and poured it over him. The whiff of the rum revived him as he tried to lift himself from the floor but fell back on to it. Finally, after many attempts, he heaved himself onto his bottom and looked around the room in bewilderment.

Contemptuously, the Backra sneered and snarled at him. As he regained control of his limbs and senses, he asked the planters why he, the King of England's general and representative on the island, was on the floor. He asked them, why they were kicking his person. The planters told him that, he had been pleading for payment and the freeing of their slaves. The general rummaged in his pantaloons and withdrew a rusty old, key which he used to open his case. He pulled out his prepared speech. As he read it, they trembled and shuddered. They seethed and fumed that their meeting had been infiltrated yet again, in the slyest of manner.

"If," they said, "these diabolical forces can control the King's general and make him speak against us; they can also enter our minds too and the minds of our families. They can get us to free them and allow them to live in our plantation houses. Surely, they will make us work in the cane pieces, as their slaves, if they get the chance," they groaned fearfully.

They huddled together to protect themselves, from the forces that threatened their dominance on their island and which they could not see or understand. Unexpectedly, the walls of the meeting room moved and shrank, threatening to squeeze them to death. It then expanded and tossed them, on top of each other, into a heap on the floor. They rolled on top of each other and screamed each time they collided. Chilling noises echoed around the room, and it forced them to cover their ears, to shut out the deafening cries of pain. All of a sudden, they were compelled to recognise for the first time, the excruciating cries that they had refused to hear, daily on their plantations when their overseers and drivers whipped their slaves.

"Our slaves are right here in this room with us, how is it possible?" they asked looking at each other for answers.

The wailing of the slaves grew louder and louder. They crouched and huddled together, to shut out the horrendous pain, they were now hearing in the howling of their slaves.

"It's our Blackies," they said.

"They have entered our sacred meeting place again to persecute us. However, we cannot see them, we can only hear their fraudulent bawling. Our drivers and overseers do not whip them harshly, they just prod them with the whip, to make them work a little harder and faster. That is all they do, and it doesn't hurt our slaves at all. Our Negroes pretend that they are being injured by the overseer's whip. They are such deceitful liars, they are always telling lies on us and our employees. However, we know otherwise. Our overseers and drivers only jest with them," they concluded.

"I bet it is the Obeah people, that have come amongst us once more to torment and kill us," sighed a planter.

They looked around the room, but could not see the malicious forces, that aimed to destroy them, for no rational reason.

"We are never free of our Negroes, even when we are away from our plantations. They try to poison and kill us in our homes; they burn our crops, buildings and murder our families and our employees. Now, they have entered our meetings. They have subjected us to their magic and the witchcraft of their Obeah men and women on our plantations. We must rid our cane pieces, of these wicked Negroes once and for all," they grunted.

"I bet," said another planter, shaking and quivering. "The defeats of our armies in the past have been caused by the actions of the Obeah people. When we eliminate them from our plantations, we will be able to control our slaves. We will also be able to remove, the Maroons from the mountaintops onto our plantations," he told them.

They all nodded in agreement. The planters agreed to meet the army general when he had fully recovered from his humiliating ordeal. They would return to their plantations and root out and execute the remaining Obeah people, among their slaves. This would guarantee them, victory against the Maroons in the mountains next time, as well as peace on their plantations.

At their next meeting, the planters were agitated; they peered around the room and trembled, whenever they heard their own breathing or exhalations. They listened to the governor and general intently. However, they were ready to leave the room if the duppies or ghosts of the Africans that they had recently executed, for being Obeah men and women had returned to take their revenge.

The general informed the planters that he had requested help many times from the Parliament in Britain, to fight the Maroons yet again. The response was disappointing, because of the poor results they had achieved over the years against them. The destruction of their great town in the East had not impressed the Parliament in England. The government was using its money, to fight those infernal wars with the French King and his army, to capture all the lands and resources of the world.

"Personally," he told them, "I would prefer to make a deal with the Maroon bands on the island; as it will save us, from another humiliating defeat. There are better ways to achieve our goals, than launching expensive campaigns against them. We have to be very strategic and clearing thinking at all times. War is costly and we have a history of defeat. It is time we tried a different option," he told them bluntly.

"The most effective strategy I believe is one of 'divide and rule'. Gentlemen, you and our slave traders have used it successfully, on the African coastline and interior to obtain, a never-ending supply of Negroes. You have divided, your field slaves from your house slaves. You have placed a wedge between the slaves born on the island and the ferocious Coromanti warriors from the coast," he told his seething audience.

"But most of all, you have placed the ultimate boulder between your Blackies and your Mulatto off-springs, this will always work in your, our favour. You, we have the solution to the Maroon question gentlemen," he told them with a confident and beaming smile.

"Divide and rule have worked extremely well over the last eighty-four years for us. If we had not divided and ruled on our plantations, our slaves would have driven us into the sea. Our arch enemies would be planting sugar instead of us. It has been a reliable weapon. It must continue to be our weapon of choice; to maintain plantation slavery, our islands, as well as our wealth," he told them unflinchingly.

"I am reluctant to use a military strategy this time. I will just put a colossal boulder, between the Maroons in the mountains and the slaves on your plantations. I intend to recruit the Maroons to our side. Then, we can use them to keep our enemies off our island and return the runaways and rebel leaders to your plantations. Your Negroes will think before leaving your plantations, for the mountains. This course of action will ensure, our total control of this and all our other islands forever," he vowed.

The planters jumped to their feet in disbelief and bounced around the room.

"First, you speak on behalf of our slaves, and now you refuse to drag the Maroons out of their mountaintop pinnacles and place them on our plantations. We have not heard, such foolish talk in a long while," they spat out at him.

"We pay you to take the war to the Maroons and return our runaway slaves to us, and that is what we expect and demand from you. We want to see military action against the savages in the mountains, or else we will abandon our plantations and invite our arch-rivals and their accomplices to take them," they told him aggressively.

They left the meeting to consider the options open to them. The army general and governor met to perfect their plan for the resistance in the mountains. The governor had listened intently to the general. However, his revenues were depleted. The government at home was reluctant to finance another war against the Maroons. They would only do so if they were sure that the Maroons would be removed from the mountain and onto the plantations.

That evening, over a sumptuous dinner, of boar's meat and rum at the governor's residence, they planned their campaign against the rebels in the mountains. They would give the planters what they asked for, as long as they paid for the campaign. I hurried to the Western mountains to inform the rebel Africans of their plans.

CHAPTER 12

The Maroons defend their ancient settlements

I, Anancy, man and spider, returned to the governor's office. I spun a web among the existing cobwebs on and between the rafters that housed the croaking lizards and the other insects that shared their home with the governor and his administration. The governor and the general, agreed on a vigorous military campaign against the rebels in the mountainous landscape, to reassure the whining planters. This strategy would also purge the mountainsides, of Nanny's armies, as well as end the rebellions on their plantations. Then, he hinted that his secret plan had to remain a secret, as he had not put the final touches to it. He reminded the governor of the strange happenings at their recent meetings. He was not convinced, that the planters had, or could remove from their plantations all the Obeah people that lived among their slaves.

However, he assured him that his plan would not be as costly, as a military campaign against the rebels. He told him that his plan would give the administration and the planters their much-desired goals. The objectives they had tried to achieve since the Blackies that they had enslaved arrived on the islands and the mainland and fled to the mountains and interior out of their control.

Forcefully, and silently, I stalked him. I implored him with every spidery muscle in my body, to voice his secret plan for the Maroon armies in the mountains. The general was resigned to the fact, that he and his army would be defeated again. Yet, he smiled knowingly as he pondered the plan, which he would not divulge, even to the King of England's representative on the island.

I returned to the mountains to inform Captain Cudjoe, of their plan to attack and destroy the Maroon settlements in the West, one by one, as they had done in the East five years previously.

"Well done Anancy, with your information we will be ready for them when they come to return us to the plantations," Captain Cudjoe replied.

"Long live Anancy," a cry went up from the Maroon warriors.

"Have I ever told you the story of Anancy and the red coats," I said with a broad grin.

"Tell us again Anancy, it will help us to prepare for the battles to come," they all laughed with glee.

Then our brave and valiant Captain Cudjoe addressed us.

"We know from the attack on our great town five years ago, that the British Army was able to destroy it, with their new-fangled weapons. We don't know how they found our settlement, but they did. We will have to make sure, they do not find any more of our great towns. We must keep them out of the mountain settlements. We must take the battle to them when the time comes. We will move down to the lower levels, we must make camps in the openings and inlets among the rocks; 'attacking first' has always been the best form of defence. They won't expect us. They hope we will remain in our towns and wait for them, then they will try and destroy it, as they did in the East," he warned them.

"Our dear brother, Anancy and our scouts, have brought us vital information to aid our planning; we know the general and governor have more than one goal for us this time. We must prepare ourselves for whatever they bring on the day. Fortunately, we have excellent scouts and an exceptional spy in the form of our brother, Anancy. We can also rely on him to infiltrate our enemies' most secret meetings, without being seen," he giggled.

"Our preparation must be as thorough as always, to secure an indisputable victory. The small pathways to the cockpits and their ridges have always worked to our advantage. We know they will be here within weeks, at the start of the dry season. Our boulders will be our cannons, gunpowder and moving weapons.

We will move the giant rocks above the entrances and build additional walls of greenery, to conceal us from their soldiers. We must build small forts, between the rock face to house our weapons, food and water. We must double our army, by using our young warriors to supply us and act as our look-out and scouts. Our experienced soldiers will take the fight to the British army as they climb up the hillsides," Captain Cudjoe instructed.

"We must have several lines of defence, to stop them getting up the slopes. We must keep them on the plains and in our sight," he told them.

"We will make sure their weapons do not leave their camps or get any footing on our mountainsides to bombard us. We will send scouts to the plantations, to burn and create confusion. This will split the armies of the planters and help us as they try to defend their cane pieces," he stressed.

"Anancy, you are the most effective weapon we possess against the planters. Therefore you can move among our brothers and sisters in their cane pieces and get them to rise up against them," instructed Chief Saro-Wiwa.

The red coats assembled on the day as expected, they appeared confident of victory this time. Their success in destroying Nanny Town in the East had made them bullish. The sound of their bugle signalled their victory. Captain Cudjoe and his men moved down the mountainside. They pulled the strategically placed boulders, letting them loose above the British army, clambering up the vertical and hilly inclines. The deafening sounds of the reverberating boulders hit the rocky and spiky hillsides; they rolled down onto the red-coated soldiers, halfway up the gradient.

The soldiers screeched in terror, as they unsuccessfully tried to move out of the way of the plummeting boulders. The boulders splintered the hillsides, creating deafening roars and an army of cascading rocks on top of them. The red-coats plunged over the bolt upright cliffs and went headlong into subterranean openings. The splintering rocks continued to tumble from the hillsides; they appeared to take on a life of their own. The boulders seemed to revitalise themselves and hurled their sharp, pointed edges, again and again into the soldiers, still determined to climb the steep hill to the mountaintop. Finally, the soldiers gave up, as the boulders rose up and blocked their path. They flung their dagger-sharp edges into their bodies; before long the lifeless corpses of the red-coated soldiers were buried under an army of splintered boulders.

The remaining soldiers' terror grew, as they were chased down the hillside, by moving trees and branches. Their cowardly commanders having sent their best soldiers ahead, watched as their men were crushed and flattened, by the animated boulders. The British Army fled from the well-organised attack of the Maroons. They ran towards the plantations to find shelter, but the Africans were waiting for them. They lit the hillsides and cane pieces with their torches, forcing the commanders back into the nook and crannies of the rocky slopes. The Maroons fractured the hillsides once more, and an army of boulders fell on them; blood seeped from their crushed heads and bodies; their blood coloured the earth.

A few brave surviving soldiers raised their muskets; they fired at the Maroons, who flicked their bodies over and over, dodging their bullets. Next, some officers got hold of their bayonets and charged the Africans standing at a distance, watching the spectacle. The youthful Maroon warriors tumbled from the hills. They grabbed hold of the weapons and pushed them into their bodies. Blood trickled from their punctured abdomens, they screamed in agony and drew their last breath. The Maroons walked the bloody battlefield; they collected the gunpowder and bayonets. They poked their sharp points, into the dying and squirming soldiers. Afterwards, the warriors rounded up the soldiers and their officers and took them, prisoners.

"I will keep these important prisoners. They will be exchanged for the release of all our brothers and sisters on the plantations, now that we have defeated the British army decisively," stated Captain Cudjoe.

A Spanish church rebuilt by the British in 1714 in St Jago de la Vega, Spanish Town, Jamaica.

Later, that night by a raging campfire, the triumphant army, led by Captain Cudjoe, celebrated joyfully their defeat of the British army once more. Their celebrations did not blind them to the reality of their situation; the majority of their brothers and sisters were still on the plantations. The elders knew they had the power, to end the misery of all the enslaved Africans on the island. They debated their victory and future tactics, well into the morning with an abundance of food and drink.

The following week, Captain Cudjoe and some of the elders, camped outside the headquarters of the general. They would demand, the release of the enslaved Africans in their cane pieces. Grudgingly, they were invited in after many days. The army chief mumbled his resentful acknowledgement, of their undeniable victory over them.

"We are here to exchange your officers, for the release of all the enslaved Africans on the island's plantations. This is the terms of our victory and your defeat," he informed him.

The army general laughed mockingly at the courageous Maroon captain.

"What are you asking of me?" he sneered.

"Do you really believe, that your victory gives you the right, to demand the freeing of the slaves on the plantations? Even if I thought they should be freed; it is not up to me. It is the decision of the planters and the King of England. I am sure you could instruct them to free the slaves, Captain Cudjoe if you wish," he said spluttering into his rum.

"If you do not free the Africans on your plantations, this war will continue. Many more plantations will be burnt. I suggest you talk to the governor and the council and persuade them to grant our request. More of your officers will die when they are let loose in the hazardous hillsides. You have a week to discuss this and give us your answer. In the meantime, we will occupy all the lowland areas around the plantations, and many of them will be burnt," he told him.

As soon as Captain Cudjoe and his men left the general's office, he summoned the planters' representative, the governor and the officials of the council. The planters' representative jeered at the army general, as they cautiously looked around the room, for evidence of their powerful and invisible persecutors.

"I guess it was too much to expect a second victory from our army," he said scoffing in his throat.

The planters cheered their representative.

"I guess our army, that has been locked in war with France to take control of the lands and resources of the rest of the world could not defeat them. Typically, our armies have only been able to burn and scatter one Maroon Town, in eighty or so years. The Maroons have defeated our military again. Our soldiers did not even get close to their camp and compounds in the mountains. How does our military expect to crush them if they cannot get up those little foothills? Our armies have allowed our slaves and the Maroons, to burn our plantations and terrify us and our families. Now, they both confidently parade and go about their business across our island and plantations. Recently, they have tried to kill us in our meetings with their Obeah people," said the representative.

The planters glared and snarled at him. The general sniggered, then he calmed himself and addressed the gathering.

"I received Captain Cudjoe and some of his chiefs this morning. He gave me an ultimatum that I know you would all like to hear. He has demanded the freeing of all your slaves within the week, for the return of my officers," he informed them.

Mayhem broke out in the room, as the general repeated the demands of the Maroon Captain. The planters paced the room in disbelief; their faces turned a plummy colour with rage and disbelief, at the request of the brazen African.

"Look the Blackies are dictating to us now," they bleated together.

"The world has gone mad. It's coming to an end. The Maroons may have defeated our army yet again, but their victory does not give them the right to demand the freeing of our slaves, that we have paid too much for in the first place. Do they think we would willingly destroy ourselves? If we freed our slaves, we would not have any plantations or comfortable incomes to live on in our stately homes in England," declared a planter.

"You can tell Captain Cudjoe, that none of our slaves will be freed. The Maroons bands and our slaves are not the same. The victory of the Maroons over our army recently, is not the victory of the slaves on our plantations," said another with scorn.

The planters' representative instructed the general and governor, to make sure the slaves remained in their cane pieces and that the Maroons joined them there.

"We must get the Maroons on our side," the general said with a widening grin.

"Then the Maroons will stay in the mountains, and they will be used to keep your slaves on your plantations," he told them.

Strutting around the room in his new found confidence, he continued in the most conceited manner.

"We will never be able to defeat the enlarged Maroon bands, that are lodged deep in the mountainous regions of the island. The Spanish will provoke your slaves to rise up, to take back this island. Our well-equipped forts around the coast, will not protect us from the Spanish armies and their swashbucklers, that intend to seize this money-making sugar island once again," he confessed.

"I will repeat my proposal again, that you all scorned at our last meeting. We must make a treaty with the Maroons, and use them to keep out our devilish enemies and their armies from our island and your plantations. We will also use them to return your runaway slaves, as well as their rebel leaders. It will be very difficult to get them to agree to a treaty. However, I have not been idle, since our recent defeat by the Maroon armies. We cannot beat them on the battlefield; therefore, we must find another way to let them forget about your slaves and concentrate on their own affairs," he sniggered.

"My contingency plan has already been put into operation. The Maroons will lose their arrogance when I am done with them. When Captain Cudjoe returns for an answer in a week's time, I will have more pressing news for him. He will be forced to choose between the survival of the Maroons or the slaves on your plantations. I can assure you all that the Maroons leaders will opt for whatever conditions we offer them. I will make Captain Cudjoe eat his words. He will need them in the coming months to feed himself and his people," he snorted and belched into his rum.

CHAPTER 13

To surrender or fight

Briskly, the children pulled up the weeds, between the yam vines that ran up the sturdy bamboo poles, jammed firmly into the ground. Increasingly, the heat of the mid-day sun had made them lethargic. They shared their small snacks, under the shade of the yam vines.

Cheekily, one of their playmates asked.

"Why do some yams have toes and feet?"

The children looked at him curiously and gave in as they saw the twinkle, in his eyes.

"Well, it was Brother Anancy who gave us yams with toes and feet," chirped their bold companion.

"How did he do that?" they asked in amazement.

Eagerly, he told them his story.

"One day some villagers dug up their yams and sent them to Kintampo yam market. The cart with the yams fell to the ground and they got mixed up. The villagers did not know which yams belonged to them because they all looked the same. They quarrelled bitterly. Eventually, the chief shared out the yams between them. However, many villagers were still very unhappy because they believed they got fewer yams, and, therefore, less money for their crop."

"Guess who walked by then," giggled the mischievous storyteller.

The children considered very carefully, they could not think of an answer so they gave in once more to the delight of the storyteller.

"Anancy, of course," he chuckled.

"Brother Anancy advised the villagers to put their feet in the yam mounds and press the number of toes they wanted firmly into the ground, before putting in the yam heads or seeds. The yams would grow, with the number of toes pressed into the mounds. This way they would know their yams whatever happened. The villagers were so delighted with Anancy's suggestion, that when they harvested their huge crops, they each gave him their biggest yam with many toes. He took the yams home and stored them in a huge grain store. Anancy, Sister Anancy and their children's bellies did not rumble from that day onwards.

"This is how yams got toes and feet," grinned the storyteller.

Remembering, they still had rows and rows of yam mounds to weed before sundown, the children attacked them. They imagined their favourite meal of pounded yams, plantains and sweet potatoes when the vines dried on the yam hillocks. The meal would be served with the tasty smoked meat of the wild boar.

Suddenly, their vigorous efforts were disrupted, as vicious dogs snarled at them and growled fiercely. The children dropped their play sticks, as they ran towards their homes and parents. They ran so fast that they did not see the events taking place behind them.

The Miskito Indians and their dogs moved across the yam fields. Savagely, they pulled up the vines from the sturdy poles, as they moved along the mounds. They trampled on the little hills, exposing the maturing yams, now squashed by their rampage. Within minutes, the carefully tended yam fields of the children and their families were tangled and wilted heaps.

Joining the parents and elders, we ran towards the yam fields. The terrified children fell into their parents' arms, begging for protection and a safe refuge, from the sharp, menacing teeth of the dogs. We saw the destruction of our crops, torn from the ground, miles and miles of yams uprooted by the bronzed Indians and their dogs. We had never seen these Indians before in the mountains, on the plantations, or in any other part of the island. We consoled each other and wondered how long it would take to restore our yam and plantain-walks. We deliberated on how we would feed ourselves and our families in the days, weeks and months to come.

Deafeningly, the ferocious dogs barked across the usually quiet and industrious valley clearing. They alerted the remaining Maroons and elders, to the scale of the attack on their provision grounds. Across the hillsides, the extensive yam fields of the brave warriors and people were being destroyed by the Miskito Indians and their dogs, as they moved through the fields trampling and uprooting the crops. The Maroon armies fired on them, to halt the destruction of their provision grounds. However, the fierce dogs that had so effortlessly scaled the ridges and valleys forced them to abandon their weapons and take cover. The sheer number of Miskito Indians and their dogs outnumbered the warriors. They refused to engage in close fighting. The dogs had kept the Maroon fighters at a distance.

Efficiently, the Miskito Indians and their dogs, moved through the precipitous cliff faces and the valleys beneath them, in search of more provision grounds further afield to destroy. The Maroon army and the inhabitants understood clearly the power of these Indians and their dogs. The general had brought them to the island, to force them to make peace.

The elders and Captain Cudjoe took stock of the destruction, of their provision grounds. They took comfort in the fact, that their great town had not been discovered. The planters and their armies had been infuriated by Captain Cudjoe's demand for the freeing of their slaves. They knew they could not guard all their provision grounds which were remote, but within the reach of those who were determined, to remove them from their sanctuaries and place them on their plantations.

The army general, the governor and the officials of the council, met Captain Cudjoe and the Maroon elders. They told them bluntly that their victory over them did not give them the right, to demand the freeing of their slaves. The Maroon elders were impertinent, so they had paid a high price for trying to dictate to them and their government. They stressed that the Blackies in their cane pieces on this island, as well as all their other islands, were their property and they would never be freed.

Then, they demanded that the Maroons help them and their army secure the island from the constant threat, from their rivals. This was the price they said they had to pay, to maintain their freedom, autonomy and peace in their mountaintop refuges. Enthusiastically, the army general addressed Captain Cudjoe; he congratulated him on his splendid victory over his army. He grinned broadly and shook his hand firmly. Then, he reminded him of the recent destruction, of nearly all of their provision grounds, by the Miskito Indians.

He informed the Maroon Elders and Captain Cudjoe that the destruction of their food crops by the Indians was an excellent reason why they should sign a peace treaty. He stressed that the Indians and their dogs would be kept on the island. They would be used against them in the future if the peace treaty was not signed.

Captain Cudjoe, I and the Maroon council, retired to their mountaintop sanctuary, to discuss their grave dilemma. But before they made their decision, I attempted to calm their rage, at the situation that they were being forced into, by the deceitful British army general and governor.

The angry countenances of the elders brightened a little, as the familiar antics of the spider so dear to them, floated in and out of their consciousness. Their minds raced to find answers to the serious decision they had to make imminently. Fervently, they hoped that the spider tales would give them the strength and courage to make the only decision they must make. The Calabash bowls with the strong smelling local brew passed around the circle. The seasoned and roasted flesh of the boar complimented the pungent drinks that calmed and prepared them for nightly tales. The night's deliberation would give them the only decision they so desperately wanted to make. In their tormented sleep and dreams, the sweet and soothing voice of their beloved spider filled their awareness during their repose.

One day I began. One day a male dragonfly, searched high and low for his beautiful mate. Recently, they had got together. He had gone out to find some decorative materials, to build their nest. The female dragonfly had gone out, too, to find the most delicate scent to perfume it. Unfortunately, some inexperienced honey thieves had stolen a honeycomb, from high in a nearby tree. The bee family besieged the thieves, as they grabbed the honey-filled comb. It fell to the ground; the delicious smelling liquid was scattered all around. The sweet smell floated into the air. The inquisitive dragonfly was drawn to the honey, she swooped down to investigate and taste it.

Her beautiful wings got stuck in the sticky liquid, as she bent down to sample it. She pulled and pulled to free herself, but her body came away from her trapped wings. She could not fly, slowly she died from hunger. Along came a little ant, he saw the crisp remains of the dragonfly. The ant was sad at the death of such a beautiful creature, but quickly realised that the body would feed his starving colony. He pulled off one of the dragonfly's leg and dragged it to his colony. Soon a swarm of industrious ants in a single file proceeded to the sticky honey trap. Skilfully and reverently, the multitude ripped apart the crisp dead body of the dragonfly, and in a lengthy procession, they took it home to store and consume.

The male dragonfly had searched high and low for his mate. One day, he found the wings of his beloved faded and worn, but still stuck in the honey. He saw an ant straining to pull a piece of it from the sticky trap. The distressed dragonfly flew at him. He accused him of killing his companion and stealing her body and now her wing. Furiously, the grieving dragonfly went in pursuit of the ant. It dodged in and out of the grains of sand. Nearby, a colony of ants saw the actions of the dragonfly; they rushed to the aid of their distressed relative. They swarmed onto the dragonfly's legs and immobilised him. Soon, the family members of the ant heard of his distress, swiftly they rushed to his aid. Outnumbered, the dragonfly begged them to free his legs.

Carefully and methodically, they released him. They removed the remainder of the crisp wings from the honey and in a never-ending convoy, they carried it to the dragonfly's nest. They laid them on a huge leaf nearby. The dragonfly had the precious wings of his much-loved companion to cherish and remind him of their love.

The story of the ants, bees and the dragonflies spun in their heads as they tossed and turned in their sleep. They prayed to their ancestors, the gods of the earth, the wind, the sun and fire to assist them in this decisive battle without muskets, gunpowder as well as cannons with moving limbs.

CHAPTER 14

The debate

The elders could not and did not sleep. How could they sleep when the despicable planters and their army were trying to strip them of their hard earned victory. They had skilfully and decisively repelled and demolished the British army's campaign against them. Now, they were dictating to them. They were forcing a settlement on them which would deny their brothers and sisters on their plantations the freedom that was theirs.

Blatantly, the Maroons were told that they had to defend the island and the British government from both their external and internal enemies; if they wanted to live in peace in their cliff top shelters. It was a bitter pill to swallow and they raged against the violence of the treaty's terms that were being imposed on them.

Slowly and reluctantly, my brothers and sisters rose from their torturous dreams, in their mountaintop hideaways. The wind blew hesitantly and doubtfully on such an ill-fated day. The cocks crowed solemnly and fearfully, for a mountain people that had only one decision to make. They would decide if and how long, their brothers and sisters remained in the cane pieces, on the island.

The elder council assembled, they deliberated and rehearsed in their heads, the decision they knew they had to make. Their debate commenced after many lengthy delays. Conscientiously, I listened to the heated arguments, that went backwards and forwards and which would decide all our futures. They knew my position; it was the story of the ants and the bees.

"We have to be realistic," coaxed Elder Ajani. "Our dear brother, Anancy has tried to put us on the only path, that is open to us with his story of the ants and the bees. They worked together to protect the interests of their colonies, from all forms of attack. In his story, the small insects were united and so they finally won against all their enemies. This is the message to us in our deliberations, on the treaty offered to us by the British government and army. However, we are not ants or bees and so this will make our decision very difficult, when all considerations are taken into account," he stated gravely.

"We know that the planters are not going to give up their possessions, without an almighty fight. They will not allow us to empty their plantations. They have time on their side. They have changed their tactics and are now trying to force us to make peace, by controlling our food supplies. The gains we have achieved away from the plantations could be lost. The planters are determined, to return all of us to their plantations. Their ultimate goal is to destroy our towns and settlements in the mountains, as they did some years ago in Nanny Town," he stressed.

"But we must consider our sisters and brothers. We must think about the brutality of their existence; as our brother, Anancy has so rightly illustrated in his story of the togetherness of those tiny creatures. Our victory will be more permanent and secure when all of them are no longer on the plantations," asserted Elder Ngugi Waani Thiong Oe.

"Deeply, we care about our brothers and sisters on the plantations, but we won't help them, by allowing the planters to starve us all to death. Our brave Captain Cudjoe has spoken to them, he has demanded the release of our kinfolk on their plantations. They refused and laughed at him contemptuously. We have to be tactical. If we remain on the mountainsides, it provides a place for our brothers and sisters to run to. A sanctuary to give them the hope of freedom, whatever we agree with the governor," Elder Ajani argued.

"Our Great African Town in the East was destroyed, to drive us from our mountain refuge so that they could extend their plantations and control over this island. We were forced to move across the island, to these bottomless and battered cliff tops. They intend to force us from these vertical mountain valleys, by whatever means again if we do not consider the peace treaty they have offered. Where will we go then into the sea? The mountainous areas of this island are extensive, but they do not all provide the concealed caverns and precipices, that will keep us safe from their armies. The Miskito Indians and their dogs are permanently stationed on this island and they will be used against us," warned Elder Mandela.

"That will always be the case, the slave masters will always find the means to further their own interests. We, also have to do the same. We have choices too. We must preserve these sanctuaries, as our ancestors and the Taino people did for us. If they had given in to the Spanish and the British at the first obstacle, we would not be here today debating this shameful offer of a treaty. We have survived and become stronger because the Taino, as well as our kinfolk, welcomed our ancestors. They did not return them to the slave masters. If we give in to their demands now when we have crushed them on the battlefield, they will cut off all the routes to our brothers and sisters in their quest for freedom," warned Captain Cudjoe.

"There are thousands and thousands of enslaved Africans on the plantations on the island. The planters, their overseers, agents and their militiamen are a drop in the ocean compared to us. Together, we can easily defeat them before they get reinforcement from Barbados or Nevis. We should be discussing this as a strategy, rather than finding arguments to convince ourselves, to accept their shameful offer of a peace treaty. We must continue to fight until all our people are on the mountaintops if they wish," urged Elder Biko.

"I agree with Elder Biko, we must not sign the treaty. We have defeated the British army decisively. We must continue the war until all our brothers and sisters are free. As an elder of the Trelawny Town Maroons, like Nanny I will not sign this treaty. It does not benefit us, or the enslaved Africans in their cane pieces in any way. We must fight on until we drive the planters and their armies from the island. When we do so, we will all be free including every African in their cane fields, the big house, the pens and the store rooms," stated Elder Nkrumah.

"Our brothers and sisters will continue to run away from the plantations, whether we sign the treaty or not. It's the harsh regimes of the planters, that drive them to the mountains. If we send them back, they will return. Our brothers and sisters in the cane pieces, know and understand the situation, they will not hold it against us. They are bold and rebellious, it is the rewards of freedom which drive them to leave, and it will end plantation slavery. We have no control over those on the plantations," argued Elder Mensah.

"If we sign the treaty, it will give us time to plan and reorganise. It will give us the space to find new areas to grow food, as well as find new sources of water for the future. We do not have the guns, or ammunition to fight another long, drawn-out war with the British army. Our brothers and sisters will continue to seek their freedom in the mountaintops, whatever we do. We must ignore the exodus and let the Backra deal with it. At this moment in time, we must replant our provision grounds and reorganise ourselves," Elder Kenyatta urged.

"While they are busying trying to stop our fleeing family members, we will have time to secure our future, by rebuilding the Maroon towns that were destroyed in the East," advised Elder Kaunda.

As the elder council debated, I saw that my story of the ants and bees were lost on the majority of them. They had been blinded by their present situation, the destruction of their yam fields. Soon the elders were beginning to be convinced by the arguments that went backwards and forward between them. The elders argued that, the loss of their provision grounds and water supplies were sufficient reasons to sign the treaty.

Nanny and the elders of the Trelawny Town Maroons argued fiercely against signing any agreement with the British army and governor, particularly since they were the victors. Forcefully, they tried to impress on their fellow elders, the deviousness of the British officials and their army. These officials would promise anything because it suited them at this moment in time, but they would go back on it later. They made one last plea to their fellow Maroon elders and Captain Cudjoe.

"We know that many of you do not want to hear this, but we will put it to this council anyway. What are the governor and general going to give us that we don't already have in terms of land? What is the quality of the land we are getting? Will it be flat and fertile? Will it meet the needs of our growing population? Will we have total control over our destiny in the future? How will our legal rights be safeguarded? Who will we turn to for redress if the terms of this treaty are dishonoured? How can we turn our backs on our brothers and sisters in the cane pieces?" asked Elder Nkrumah.

"If the answers to any of these questions are doubtful, then we must not sign the treaty with the governor and his officials. We continue to fight, we are one family. Therefore, we are responsible for each other at all times," Nanny stated firmly but quietly.

Desperate to regain control of the island, the governor again urged the Maroon leaders to sign the treaty at their next meeting.

"This agreement," the governor said, in his most friendly voice, allow us to live side by side on this island in peace. You have fought for the right, to live in the mountains of this green and flourishing island. We do not require those of you in the mountains, to return to the plantations. You must understand, we cannot allow more of our slaves to leave the estates and ruin us," he admitted.

"I will restate our position, all Africans free to join us in the mountaintops if they wish," stressed Nanny.

"If we agreed to your demands, there would only be the worn out and sick left on our plantations. We know our slaves do not want to be there. They are there because we force them to be there. At this moment in time, our interests are the same. Sign the treaty or the alternative will be the destruction of all Maroon settlements, on this island in due course," threatened the governor and the army general.

"The Eastern Maroons will not sign any treaty with the planters and their government, that have made our family members slaves in their cane pieces. Colonisers that have stopped them from living as families and have also prevented them from honouring their ancestors. Slave masters that have stopped them from speaking and singing in the languages of our motherland, but most of all they have prevented them from having control of their lands," stated Nanny.

Passionately, she continued.

"The slave owners have stopped them from living as human beings, we will destroy slavery. We will not sign, come what may," proclaimed warrior Nanny defying the white slave owners.

"The choice is yours, I hope all the Maroon communities will think on it and sign the treaty very soon. Look, we control most of your water supplies; it will also take another year before any provision grounds you find to cultivate, will produce enough food to feed all your community. I promise you that as the representative of the King on this island, I will use the Miskito Indians and their dogs, to root out your remaining provision grounds. Then you will all starve to death," he laughed viciously.

After much deliberation, those elders who were weary of war and envisaged their families and themselves being starved out of their mountaintop homes voted to accept the terms of the treaty. The First Maroon Treaty was signed in 1739 by the governor of the island, stipulating its terms. The agreement stated:

Maroons in the Leeward (West) and the Windward (East) lands remain in the settlements they have fought for and are in control of, along with an additional 1500 hectares of land.

The Maroon settlements will be allocated a British Superintendent of our choice, as a liaison officer.

Maroon communities must return all runaways slaves, to the plantation from which they came.

Maroon communities must fight with the British army against the French, Spanish and Dutch monarchs, their soldiers and pirates that want to take this and the other islands controlled by us.

Maroon communities are free to organise themselves in whatever way they see fit.

Maroon communities are responsible for disciplining those elements in their communities, who do not abide by the laws set out in the treaty and their communities.

No Maroons will be transported from this island.

"I have carried out my promise, now you Captain Cudjoe as leader of the largest group of Maroons, you must sign this treaty. If you do not sign it, we will have to rid this island of all the Maroon communities before long," the governor threatened.

The Maroon armies and elders had been victorious in battle again and again against the British army and planters. However, it was the slave masters who won the war. The general's plan had worked. They had set us against each other, by getting some Maroon leaders to sign their treaty. This agreement required them to police their brothers and sisters on their plantations and return them to the very conditions they had fled from; and which they had fought so ferociously not to go back to.

The Maroon communities in the mountains gave the planters the time and opportunity to tighten their grip on, their family members in their cane pieces. Now, they would extract even more labour from them because they had divided them. The planters had secured their future and prosperity, without any significant threat from the largest Maroon community on the island for the time being.

The enslaved Africans on the plantations knew they could not depend on their family members in the cliff top settlements to free them; therefore, they had to free themselves. However, it was not long before the planters, realised that it was the Blackies on their plantations, who presented the greatest threat to them. They threatened their wealth, power and control of their island and islands.

CHAPTER 15

Rebellions at home and abroad

The British army and planters were deliriously happy with the signing of the treaty. They had engineered a peace treaty, even though they had been humiliated, by the Maroons on the battlefield. They congratulated themselves on their remarkable achievement. The Maroons were now firmly fixed to the mountaintops and the routes out of their plantations were now securely sealed against their slaves. They had secured their incomes and their future forever.

Indeed, many of our family members in the mountains had abandoned their brothers and sisters on the plantations, to preserve their own individual freedoms, in their ancient settlements. However, the elders of the Trelawny Town Maroons, who had argued so fiercely against signing the treaty, would not turn their backs on their brothers and sisters. Clearly, they saw the limitation of the agreement. They knew it was conceived, to serve the interests of the planters and their government solely.

They had moved further west, to the far-flung corners of the Cockpit Country, to set up their own communities. The Trelawny elders knew that the Africans in the mountaintops were not free. They were free to roam and live in the rocky outcrops as well as returning their brothers and sisters to the planters' cane pieces. Their so-called freedom was a delusion, which they had to confront daily. So they had taught the youth, the importance of continuing the struggle for the total liberation of all Africans in 'The Enslaved World'. When the elders passed on, the young men and women took up the challenge and resisted the actions of the planters and government which breached the 1739 treaty.

Rebellions on the islands and on the mainland erupted every year after the agreement was signed. The overseers had increased their surveillance of the enslaved Africans, to put down conspiracies and plots before they became major rebellions. Yet, they failed to detect and prevent many of the frequent uprisings on their plantations in these years. Twenty years, after the treaty was signed one of the biggest insurrection on the island broke out in the parish of St Mary. Rapidly, it spread across the island and especially to the Western parish of, Westmoreland. Thousands of enslaved Africans rose up again to end their enslavement. They were led by an overseer named Tacky. Tacky's rebellion challenged every planter on the island and beyond. The enslaved Africans, led by their chief burnt and took over many plantations on the island. For several months, the planters and their armies feared for the future of their island. They could not crush the rebellion or its leaders. The Backra knew that they would be driven from the island. The administration knew that they had to find the person directing the uprising swiftly; they hoped this would restore their authority and control over their island.

In desperation, they summoned the Maroon captains from their mountaintop sanctuaries. They reminded them, of the terms of the 1739 treaty and ordered them, to find the rebellion's leader. The Maroon trackers tramped through the hills and mountaintops in search of him. The enslaved Africans, on the plantations, hid him in the nook and crannies of their compounds and their secret places. They were always one step ahead of the Maroon trackers and the British army. Frustrated by the lack of progress in finding him, the governor and general called in all the Maroon captains for the second time. They ordered them to find him immediately.

Eventually, after many months, the Africans had no more secret places to hide Tacky, from the army of Maroon trackers searching for him. On a fateful day, a Maroon tracker saw Tacky; he stalked him throughout the day. At dusk, he trailed him to his resting place. As Tacky looked about him and prepared to rest

On EASTER SUNDAY, in the year 1760 in this Parish, the great rebel leader named Tacky led our ancestors in a rebellion against the slave owners. They raided the English garrison at Fort Haldane and attacked the estates, Frontier, Trinity, Ballard's Valley, Esher, among others. Tacky's revolt spread to several parishes before it ended. The brave Tacky lost his own life but he had struck a blow for freedom that helped to hasten the end of bondage.

JAMAICA NATIONAL TRUST COMMISSION.

A monument to Tacky outside the Parish Library in Port Maria, Jamaica.

his weary head, he was unaware of the Maroon tracker close by; he laid his head on the exposed and trailing roots of a huge Guango tree. The Maroon tracker shot him; very quickly he cut off his head and took it to the governor to claim his thirty pieces of silver. Promptly, he took the head and placed it on a spike. He paraded it around the square in Spanish Town and left it on display during the day. That night Tacky's foot soldiers took it down; they buried it with a traditional African ceremony, suitable for a brave African resistance fighter. Tacky had used his privileged position as an overseer to resist the planters and he had tried to end Plantation slavery on the island for everyone.

Tacky's disciples continued the struggle to end their enslavement; they moved west and challenged the planters and their armies for some time. The planters had pacified some Maroons, but there were many, many determined enslaved Africans who would continue to defy them daily in the hilly terrain of their island. The planters, the governor and the army now understood, that the treaty with the Maroons had not diminished the threat to plantation slavery and themselves. Daily, it had not stopped many enslaved Africans from fleeing from their plantations and rising up against their authority and power.

As the years passed, many of the Trelawny Town Maroons continued to suffer from the violations of the 1739 treaty. Continuously, successive governors and their administrations continued to ignore the terms of the agreement. They refused to listen to the grievances of all the Maroons, including the Trelawny Town Maroons. They could not get the redress they were entitled to. The treaty had stipulated that the Maroons were to be disciplined within their own communities. Subsequent, governors and their officials ignored this clause. They punished Maroons time and time again in public, for trivial or invented incidents. This demonstrated clearly to the youthful Maroons, the weaknesses in the settlement.

The land allocated to them could no longer sustain the new generations of Maroons and the enslaved population, who joined them in the mountains, because of its diminishing fertility. There had been no provision in the treaty to increase their acreage over the years. Successive governors had ignored their request for more fertile and productive land. They threatened to transport, many young Maroons from the island because they said they were plotting with the rebels in St Domingue and the enslaved Africans in their cane pieces, to drive them from their island.

The British army and governor were extremely anxious and troubled. Once again, they felt the challenge to their control of their island, from the young Maroons as they demanded that they abide by the terms of the settlement. They watched with trepidation as the African rebels, and their generals in St Domingue confronted the French administration and armies and defeated them time and time again. They trembled and imagined, the young Maroons in secret meetings with the agents of the African generals in St Domingue, around the coves and inlets of their island.

The planters and the council had had to rescue many French planters from St Domingue. These fleeing plantation owners had brought their slaves with them. The fearful British government quickly locked them up, to prevent contact with their slaves. Of course, I, Anancy, could not miss such a superb opportunity. I sneaked into the prison, which held the Africans from St Domingue. I learnt in detail, of the campaign and organisation of their General Toussaint L'Ouverture and our brothers and sisters to rid the island of the French government and planters. I passed it on to my enslaved brothers and sisters as well as the youthful Maroons.

From 1492 onwards, the Taino, the Amerindians and later the Africans, had begun the fight for freedom, equality, justice and liberation from the Backras' cane pieces. They had initiated and led the struggle for self-determination, in 'The Recently Enslaved World', for themselves and those in the Old World too. As their resistance to their enslavement intensified, they saw the principles and practices they had been fighting for recognised. These were enshrined in the American war and the declaration of independence in 1776 and much later in the decrees of the French Revolution between 1789 and 1794. They had led the struggle for human dignity, freedom and equality for centuries.

As the years passed, the young Maroons intensified their guerrilla war against the planters to redress their mounting grievances. The slave masters and their government vowed to crush forever, the Maroons' resistance. They begged their government for troops, to secure the island from the young and devilish Maroons. They informed them that they were probably being financed by the Negro generals in St Domingue, but more importantly they were taking their women slaves, to the mountaintops.

Fortunately, for the youthful Maroons, the troops did not arrive immediately. It allowed them time, to plan and perfect their campaign. The British army was extremely stretched as the enslaved peoples on the islands, and mainland continued to fight to liberate themselves. The British army was fighting the Black Caribs, or the Garifuna people of St Vincent, to take the island for their King. Another battalion was fighting the Spanish, to take control on the isle of Trinidad for the monarchy, to gain easy access to the South American mainland.

Other forces were stuck on the island of Grenada, fighting the enslaved Africans and their leaders, to maintain British rule on the island. Their armies were also busy, on the islands of St Lucia and Dominica, attempting to put down major slave rebellions. Another division along with the Spanish Army was trying to retake St Domingue, from the African generals for the British and Spanish royal family. They were also rebellions in Curacao, Guadeloupe, Martinique, Tortola, Demerara and Venezuela on the Caribbean coast of South America.

The rebellion in Venezuela was led by our brother Jose Chirinos. He and his African army took over the country for many, many months and declared it a Republic. This infuriated the Spanish King; he sent his regiments to put down the rebellion, our brave brother Jose was killed. Many of our brothers and sisters were also slaughtered as a lesson to those Africans, on their plantations intent on liberating themselves. The French, Spanish, Dutch and British armies were extremely busy.

Finally, the British king heeded the request of the governor and the planters. He redirected his armies to reassure the colonisers and keep his money supply and colony.

CHAPTER 16

The undefeated Maroons?

Again, the planters gathered in the governors' office in Spanish Town. They praised and toasted, the Maroons elders who had abided by the 1739 treaty. The Maroons had rescued them, from the devilish Tacky and his army of spiteful Negroes. They had prevented a revolution, which would definitely have swept them from their island. They concluded that the island would be a much happier place if the young and reckless Trelawny Town Maroons in the Cockpits would follow the exemplary behaviour of the older Maroon elders and their communities. Now, they could carry on making money, without further disruptions.

However, it was not long before their contentment, again gave way to groans and anxiety, about the continued resistance of the youthful Maroons. Their representative again voiced their concerns.

"Over the years, the Trelawny elders have encouraged their youth to question the terms of the 1739 treaty, that we have implemented scrupulously. We have been extremely honourable and fair in carrying out our responsibilities as set out in it. However, they have continued to terrorise us as well as our families because they question our execution of the settlement. Frequently, they enter our cane pieces, they burn and disrupt them. They carry off dozens of our women slaves, to their mountaintop precipices.

Soon, we will not have any slaves left on our plantations to grow sugar. The survival of our cane pieces is in great danger. It is rumoured that future laws might stop the transportation of slaves in our ships. We sincerely hope and pray, that this will not come to past. If it happens, we will have to buy expensive Negroes, from our rival slave traders. The cost will cripple us and our plantations. Then, we will have to watch helplessly as the youths, raid our cane pieces and take them from us," the representative groaned.

Then the governor addressed them.

"It is a problem we must deal with right away. We need a contingency plan so that if our ships are banned from carrying slaves, our livelihood is not threatened, whatever Parliament decides. From now on, we must use the slave women to breed even more slaves, not only for the big houses but for our cane pieces too, this will offset the immediate threat to our future. It is also vital that we stop the young Maroons now. The French threat to our colony has subsided for the time being, as they try to retake their island from those Negro Generals masquerading as military men. This is a god sent opportunity to crush them without delay," he concluded.

"I agree with you sirs, these Maroons are young and unseasoned in warfare. This will make defeating them a lot easier. Fortunately, for us the majority of the Maroons will abide by the 1739 treaty. They will not fight with the Trelawny Town youths against us. Our ships are off the coast, we must begin our campaign," the general advised them.

They applauded in agreement.

"Our preparations are complete, shortly we will proceed to the Cockpits once again. Our God will be with us. We will build forts around their settlements so that we will not be sitting targets for their fighters when we enter those treacherous cliff tops," he told them.

"Firstly," he said, "we will place our army and the imported Miskito Indian trackers around their settlements. Secondly, we will set fire to the surrounding mountains and countryside if they try to escape. Thirdly, we have found and burnt most of their provision grounds and disrupted their water supplies. Fourthly, our ships are stationed off the coast, with some of their most respected warriors and elders, which we captured earlier.

They are our prisoners and our insurance. The ship will sail to North America after we have crushed them. Finally, we will have the option of using the Cubans and their ferocious tracker dogs if they defeat us which, I assure you, will not happen. With these strategies in place and their inexperience, we can be sure of victory this time," the new and ambitious general assured himself and his assembled audience.

I, Anancy, and the youthful Maroons had planned our campaign to the smallest detail; we were ready for them. Our morale was boosted, by the news of the continuing success of the African Generals and people against the French army in St Domingue. Tirelessly, I worked with them as they were the only group of Maroons, who had continued to respond to the disrespect shown, by successive British officials and their administrators for the 1739 contract. I scaled the cliff tops into the British forts, with the young scouts to look at their weapons and plans for us. I also knew our food and water supplies, would be destroyed as in the 1739 war. We sought and found alternative sources of water and food.

At the end of the rainy season, the British army climbed the vertical mountainsides into the Cockpits, with their great weapons. Their scouts had told them that, the Maroon armies were there waiting to engage them. They waited and waited for them to leave their mountain caves. The general assured his men that they were trapped. Knowing that they would use their enormous cannons on them, they had emptied their towns. The people had been moved to the ancient Maroon settlements, in the mountains in the middle section of the island and back to the East.

The young and energetic Maroons had dug through the limestone walls, linking the caves, until they had the longest tunnels with many exits beyond the caves and out of the reach of the British army's weapons. They moved in and out of their tunnels of safety. Time and time again, they used their hit and run tactics against the British army, with great success. The weeks and months dragged by, they were exhausted.

However, their youthfulness sustained their desire to drive the planters and their armies from the island, so they could live healthy and rewarding lives. The tunnels of protection allowed them, to keep up their attacks on the British army and retreat into their subterranean limestone places of security.

Drained by the long drawn out war, that sapped their men and ammunition, the British general sent for the one hundred Cuban tracker dogs and their handlers to sniff them out.

The youthful Maroons and their elders knew that they were at a critical point in the war. They would have to defeat the British army swiftly. Their tunnels would not protect them forever. They had to act now if they were to remain free and in control of their lives. They made one last plan with their senior Anancy. They would leave their safe haven and confront the eager and well-equipped British army with their heavy guns and cannons. They devised a cunning plan to trap them. Carefully, they chose and prepared the ground on which they would engage the British troops. On the day of the combat, the British soldiers chased the Maroons haphazardly with their heavy weapons over several hillocks.

The Maroons stood their ground as the militia came closer and closer and aimed their enormous guns at them. Almost, like lightning they fled to the higher ground. The general ordered his officers and troops to blast them out of the Cockpits forever. The artillerymen were forced to haul their heavy guns over the bumpy hills in pursuit of them. The Maroons would not get away this time, their heads would stand guard in Spanish Town to show their Negroes their fate if they continued to plot and scheme with their enemies. The artillerymen took up a tug of war formation and dragged their cumbersome and clumsy field gun over the hilly ground to follow the agile Maroons.

The youths made one last dash to an elevated peak. The confident British soldiers lugged their heavy weapons after them. As the army aimed their cannon and fired at the young fighters perched on the hill, the earth opened up and their bulky equipment and some of the militia fell through. Straightaway, the

A cannon outside a British administrative building in Spanish Town, Jamaica.

Maroons disappeared and claimed the sinking weapon. The British army realised they had been tricked, they fled down the bumpy hillside. Without delay, the Maroons heaved the gun to the top of the hill and waited until the British army was in sight and fleeing. They fired on them using their own weapon. The British soldiers and officers sunk into the hillside as the gunpowder and balls of iron shattered their bodies. The few surviving soldiers and their general flew from the battlefield and were very, very silent.

We were the victors; we were undefeated. We had won the battle.

We celebrated boisterously in our watery caves. We had slaughtered them on the battlefield and it could not be denied. Our people had returned to the cliff tops to celebrate our victory. Together we began rebuilding our community. The humiliated army general had been working hard to move through the ranks to become the next governor. We had destroyed his aspirations.

We were unaware that, after their unquestionable defeat the general had speeded up the landing of the Cuban dogs on the island and intended to use them against us. Swiftly and secretly, they sprinted to our cliff top compounds. Soon, our mountain sanctuary was surrounded by the Cuban dogs and their handlers. They had scaled the vertical mountainsides into our refuge. We were unprepared; the general ordered them to destroy us. They savaged us, our families and our community. We could not hide from their sharp and destructive teeth.

The general stood aloof from our wounded compounds. He ordered us to surrender and sign a peace treaty. He mocked us and told us that our victory over his army had been very, very brief indeed. The British Army were the victors now, they had won the war. We knew we had slaughtered them weeks before on the battlefield. However, history was repeating itself, the Maroons' victory over the planters and their armies was once again turned against them, their achievement in war would be used to continue their enslavement.

Our brutalised communities and captured fighters were now our priority. The Maroon elders signed the peace treaty, but that wasn't enough because we had humiliated and defeated them. The general rounded up five hundred Maroons and shipped them along with their captured fighters to cold and frozen Nova Scotia. They burned their great town to erase their history of resistance.

In Nova Scotia, the Maroons fought hard against the menial and degrading work they were forced to do along with the conditions in which they were compelled to live. The British administration there shipped them to Sierra Leone in West Africa, as the final solution to their rebelliousness. The Maroons had by their defiance, compelled the British government to send them back to Africa. They had attained their goal of a return to their motherland.

Rebellions on the plantations slowed for a time, as the routes to the mountaintops were significantly restricted by the two peace treaties. However, they picked up momentum when the enslaved Africans on the plantations learnt about the uprisings and victories of Africans, the Taino and Amerindian peoples nearer home or on the mainland. The events outside the island influenced their resistance considerably.

The Trelawny Town Maroons' conclusive defeat of the British army, on the battlefield and their return to their ancestral home, in West Africa, boosted their determination to end their enslavement.

CHAPTER 17

The women's burden

Temporarily, cut off from assistance in the mountains of hope for the second time, my brothers and sisters on the plantations fought the planters unrelentingly. They had nothing to lose. On a regular basis, plots were uncovered as my brothers and sisters strove to free themselves. The majority of them were still in bondage. However, slavery was dying and it was those who remained on the plantations, who finally brought plantation slavery to an end. As it became harder to flee the plantations, they used whatever means necessary to sabotage the planters and slave traders. The women became the greatest asset to the planters, but also the most serious threat to them and their government; especially as the dreaded Act of 1807, would end their monopoly to supply the Spanish and British colonies with enslaved peoples.

The planters and slave merchants were outraged by the implementation of the Act, as it threatened their continued existence. Hastily, the slave owners put in place their alternative strategy. The slave women became the instrument, to breed the next generation of slaves for their plantations. They decided to pay each woman a very small sum of money to have children, the payment increased if the child lived for more than nine days or if they gave birth to more than one child. The women did not comply. Frustrated and in a panic, about the lack of newborn babies on their plantations, they drew up lists of young women to breed the next generation of slaves. Again, they offered them trivial rewards, to have many children. Vigorously, my sisters resisted the planters' plans to make them produce the next generation of free labour for their cane pieces.

In order to ensure their survival, the planters made up great lists of women who were forcibly impregnated. The women rebelled, and the embryos were never born. The women came together, to discuss the additional burden imposed on them by the planters as well as the solutions that were available to them.

"It's difficult for us to stay on the plantation when we know that there is freedom in the mountains. It's harder now for us to run away because they keep a tighter rein on us. They want to make us have even more children, to work in the big house and now in their cane pieces. It is a system that degrades us and destroys our family life. We are forced to breed. Our children will be taken from us and used to continue our enslavement. How can we be happy to give birth to an army of children, to maintain plantation slavery?" asked Nzinga.

The women nodded in agreement.

"The Backra will take our children to market and sell them throughout the island as well as across the seas after we have carried them for nine months," sighed Buchiemeche.

"Our babies will be taken to the cane pieces before they are old enough. Daily, our children, will be fed on the scraps from the planters' table. We and our children are merely commodities to the planters, to maintain their wealth, power and control over us. The Backra cannot make us have babies, no matter how many times they send us to be impregnated or rape us. We will use the medicine and Obeah people to make sure our children will not be the pillars of the plantations in the future," the women concluded.

"We will only have children if we want them and can give them a good family life and teach them, to become moral as well as generous human beings," declared Wangarim.

"I will run away to the mountains, again and again, to make sure my children are not born, to maintain this monstrous system," Nefertiti told them.

"Four young women fled last week. Two of them ran away after they informed their sick mistress, they were going to find herbal plants to cure her illness, and they have not returned," explained Makeda.

Kemi, a tall woman, asked in Twi if they had heard the story of 'Beauty' and her would-be Backra suitor.

Eagerly, they gathered to hear the latest story.

"Beauty dealt admirably with a newly arrived male family member, who tried to force his reckless desires on her," she told them.

"I haven't heard, when did this happen?" asked Makebamir.

Gripped, they listened to Kemi's retelling of the events.

"Last month," she told them, "a young Backra arrived from England, the heir of the plantation owner. He had come to see what he was about to inherit. He had doubts about taking over the estate because he had heard of the savagery of the Negroes. He was also aware of the oppressive weather and diseases in the tropics, that ended the lives of Europeans, as soon as they set foot on the islands and the mainland. However, he was persuaded by his uncle to visit at a pleasant time of the year. In this season, chilly breezes blew across the island and there was an abundance of flowers, fruits and vegetables," Kemi recounted.

They were gripped so she continued cheerfully.

"On arrival, he was pleasantly surprised that the Negroes were not running around naked killing the whites. This calmed his nerves. He set about observing the daily workings of the plantation. Soon, he noticed many women of great beauty. This surprised him greatly. He watched them from afar. After a while, he spoke to his uncle about his feelings towards some of these women. His uncle told him that it had been the custom of the planters, to keep a group of Negro women to work in the big house. These women's children would also work in the plantation houses when they were old enough. However, this practice would become even more essential, in the coming years to breed slaves for their cane pieces too, when British ships could no longer bring slaves to the island. There were rumours that the trade would end very soon," she indicated.

"The Negro women and their offsprings, his uncle told him were now essential for their survival. But more importantly, they provided one of the most valuable services for them; they kept them informed of any plots or rebellions that were being planned on their plantations. This was necessary, as daily their slaves planned and schemed among themselves and with their enemies abroad, to take their islands from them. The majority of their offsprings were attentive; they had allowed them to maintain their control of the island so far. This was the main reason they associated with Negro women. He also told him it was universally known and accepted, that Negro women were inferior to European women, and there was no question about it. The planters' association with Negro women, he said secured the island and plantations, for the King of England."

Then she told them some more of the insulting things he had said about them.

"He said marriage to Negro women were out of the question, they were to be used to satisfy their masters' many needs and now to produce the workforce for the future. He encouraged him to assert his authority over the women, as this would prepare him for when he took over the plantation," she shared with them.

"The very next day," she said, "he approached a woman of great beauty. Her name was 'Beauty'; he spoke forcefully to her. Beauty avoided his eyes but did not seem offended by his manner and approach; he was expectant. That night, Beauty had a word with all of us. We decided to get as much as we could, from this young and eager Backra for each other. He would feel the sting of the African woman. She spoke sweetly to him the next day. She told him of the distress of the children and the elders. Politely, she asked him if he could help them get some supplies, which would improve their health as well as allowing them to live better," she disclosed.

"She also spoke to our brother Anancy about her dilemma, and they talked about possible solutions. She begged him to help her deal with this very tricky situation. She did not want to antagonise the Backra too much, as he may seek revenge when he took over the plantation. They talked and talked and then together they devised a plan to humble the young Backra."

"Next day, she spoke to him in her gentlest and most courteous voice. She arranged a meeting under a huge Tamarind tree, by a stream. As the sun set, the fresh evening breeze floated across the plantation yard, the eager young Backra walked at speed to the Tamarind tree laden with gifts. He gave her a very shiny one that he had bought in a Liverpool store. It was a plain metal bracelet. He said he was sure she would treasure it forever," she told them.

"Once the gifts were presented, he jumped onto his beloved. Suddenly, four hairy arms came towards him while the beautiful face of his Beauty turned into a hairy black spider. At the same time, his body itched; his skin was covered with hundreds of black insects. Noticing a stream nearby, he threw himself into it scratching and screaming. He was rescued by his family and confined to the house, before his prompt return to England. His family could not make head or tail, of his account of the meeting under the Tamarind tree. They concluded that the weather had got the better of him. Maybe, he was not the best person to take over the plantation if he could not assert his authority and power over the slave women," she informed them.

"Next day, we all met Beauty and our brother, Anancy, under the tree. We laughed at the folly of the young Backra as we shared the spoils. But our high spirits were spoilt, by the knowledge of the continued suffering of all our sisters on the plantations, across the islands and the mainland. As women, we work in the cane pieces, we farm our small plots growing food, to feed ourselves and our children. Each day, we worried about those family members that were taken from us, as well as those who would be stolen in the future and sold across the seas. We live in constant fear, of rape along with the abuse of our bodies, to produce workers for their plantations, or satisfy their perverted desires," Kemi admitted.

We also reflected on our own situation, as enslaved peoples on the plantation.

"We women, men and children, are all victims of this harsh and brutish regime. We have to intensify our efforts, to maintain the firm bonds that exist between our compounds and the cane pieces. We must work hard not to lose contact with our family members, wherever the planters send them. We must not be divided by the false affections, trinkets and presents that the Backra use to break our loyalty to each other. By everyone working together, women, men and children, we will defeat slavery. We must at all times, teach our brothers as well as our children that strength lies in unity. We must shun the practices of the Maroons in the mountaintops, who have returned their brothers and sisters to the planters. They have destroyed our drive to liberate every enslaved African in the cane pieces in the islands and on the mainland," stated Beauty.

"The slave masters and their government have consistently placed a wedge between the free Africans and ourselves. They have also put a barrier, between us in their cane pieces and those in the big house. This is how they have maintained plantation slavery and their control over us. They have been and are the only beneficiaries of slavery," sighed Yennega.

I, Anancy, agreed and comforted my sisters with soothing words, that I knew would not protect them from the depravity, greed and perverted nature of the Backra and their agents.

"We have worked together since our enslavement, to bring about our emancipation," I told them. "We will continue to do so until slavery and suffering no longer exist on the islands and the mainland or in any part of the world. I know that many of us are guilty of taking on the behaviour of the planters and this hinders our struggle to be free. I know that you all suffer greatly. Constantly, you are the victims of untold abuse, by the planters and many times at the hands of our own brothers. We must stand against all tyrants," I told them.

"You have been an excellent brother to us Anancy. You have consoled and reassured us when we have been in great despair. You have helped us to grow strong, to fight this system that daily rapes and degrades us and shorten our lives with excessive work. We have been able to come to you and talk about our severe hurt and pain. We have smiled when you have tried to lighten our sorrow, by making us laugh with your antics," they said affectionately.

CHAPTER 18

The end of slavery?

The enslaved Africans were now alone with the Backra on their plantations. Now, they had nothing to lose but the visible and invisible chains that shackled them to the plantations; as well as the drivers and overseers' whips, that disfigured their half-clothed and half-starved bodies.

Gradually, the Backra were forced to rethink their plans, after the abolition of the carrying of slaves in British ships in 1807 and also because of the continued resistance, of the enslaved Africans. Breeding slaves for their plantations became the Backras' new obsession. Reluctantly, they modified their strategies and attitudes towards the Africans, to meet head-on the latest threat to plantation slavery and their continued existence.

The planters had used the Catholic and Protestant religions, to justify the brutal enslavement of the Africans, their exclusion from their churches and a natural family life. Progressively, they began to abandon these justifications. Soon, they began to discuss the advantages to themselves, of bringing the Bible and its teachings to their Blackies. Enthusiastically, a few Backra extracted passages from the Bible, that promoted a stable family life, as well as the breeding of children. They forced this onto their slaves. They had always controlled the Africans' body with the whip, why not their minds too with their religion, now that it suited them?

Hence, many of the fearful planters swallowed the bitter pill. They ordered their overseers, not to work their slaves to death any longer or hurl African families to the four corners of the islands and the mainland. Now, they made it compulsory, for the enslaved Africans to go to church on their only full day away from their cane pieces. Their attendance at church, as well as the randomly reconstructed African family; would ensure that they would multiply abundantly, thus guaranteeing their future by mass producing children to work in their cane pieces. They rewarded them with trivial gifts if they agreed to be baptised into their religious faiths and breed endlessly.

Forcefully, my brothers and sisters rejected the faith and religion of the planters, as well as their plans to make them uphold plantation slavery. They chose the Baptist and Moravian churches instead. These religious denominations had opposed plantation slavery and supported the Africans in one form or another, from their arrival on the islands. Many Africans embraced these faiths. They took from them those characteristics, which facilitated their route out of the plantations and complimented the world view of the continent they had been snatched from. The enthusiastic Africans celebrated their three precious days of holiday at Christmas. They honoured the birth of their God, in the religious faiths that had recognised and accepted them as human beings. Deacon Sharp addressed his immaculately dressed congregation, who were eager to make the most of their favourite holiday, away from the Backras' cane pieces.

"Temporarily, but only temporarily brothers and sisters, the shackles and chains have been lifted from our hands and feet. This means that today we are free to pray to and celebrate, the birth of the true Lord God, our Saviour Jesus Christ," he said.

"Amen, Amen," replied the eager congregation.

"God and our ancestors have brought us to this day. They have stood with us, as the drivers and overseers' whips, ate into our flesh in their cane pieces. They have stood with us when our children and loved ones were ripped from us and sold to yonder plantations. They have stood with us when our young women have been raped and brutalised by the Backras' lust. They have been with us when we have fled the plantations to seek our freedom, on the rock-solid and jagged mountainsides. This God is a just God, unlike the God of the slave masters. Today, this

137

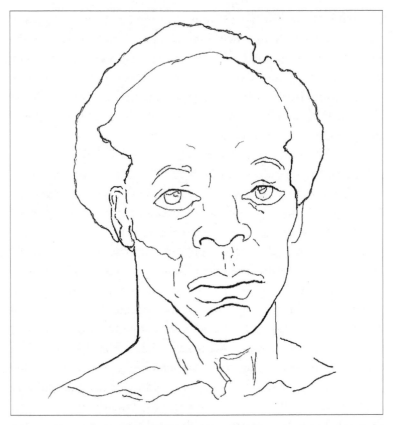

Sam Sharpe, leader of the Christmas Rebellion of 1831, and a Jamaican National Hero, from the official portrait.

holy and extraordinary day, he and our ancestors stand with us in our great affliction," Deacon Sharp told his flock.

"Halleluiah, halleluiah, praise the Lord our God," replied the churchgoers.

Noisily, they continued.

"He is an impartial God, he is a righteous God, he is a just God and we are all his children," they recited.

"We must worship and praise our Lord God, on the three beloved days that we have at this time of the year. We must not work on any of these days; they are holy and our only days of rest and renewal. Christmas falls on a Sunday this year, our only full day of restfulness. It is our day. We must demand a day instead for it, or be paid for working on the day after the end of our three priceless days. These are our days to do what we want with them. We must visit friends and family and look after the sick and needy in our compounds. We must use these glorious days to reunite and bond with all our many families on the island. We must get pleasure from the only three days, in the year when we can come together as Africans, without the fear of the overseers and drivers' whips," he stressed.

"Amen, Amen," bawled the worshippers.

Purposefully, he thumped the makeshift altar and addressed his audience.

"We will not work in the cane pieces during these blessed days, or on our holiday and the birth of the true God," he counselled them.

"Will we work on these days?" he demanded.

"No, no," answered his defiant parishioners.

"Our Master is in heaven, not on this earth," roared the assembled worshippers.

"We must do God's will at all times and only when we have worshiped and honoured his name, shall we consider the wishes of our earthly masters," directed Deacon Sharp.

"Amen, amen," responded the gathering.

"It is only when we have praised and glorified his name, that we will be able to consider our earthly burdens," he told them.

"Amen, amen, amen," hollered the members of the congregation.

At nightfall, they congregated under the branches of an encompassing Guango tree, to make merry away from the cane pieces. Deacon Sharp addressed them, once again and posed the question he had asked in church earlier.

"Will we cut the ripening cane in the fields during our special holiday?" he asked.

"No, no if the Backra wants the cane cut, let him cut it himself," the revellers yelled.

"This is our sacred holiday. The planters could offer to pay us, and we might cut it on the fourth day that is rightly our holiday.

Head-Quarters, Montego-Bay,
St. James's, Jan. 2, 1832.

TO

THE REBELLIOUS SLAVES.

NEGROES,

YOU have taken up arms against your Masters, and have burnt and plundered their Houses and Buildings. Some wicked persons have told you that the King has made you free, and that your Masters withhold your freedom from you. In the name of the King, I come amongst you, to tell you that you are misled. I bring with me numerous Forces to punish the guilty, and all who are found with the Rebels will be put to death, without Mercy. You cannot resist the King's Troops. Surrender yourselves, and beg that your crime may be pardoned. All who yield themselves up at any Military Post *immediately*, provided they are not principals and chiefs in the burnings that have been committed, will receive His Majesty's gracious pardon. All who hold out, will meet with certain death.

WILLOUGHBY COTTON,
Maj. General Command[s].

GOD SAVE THE KING.

Notice addressed to "The Rebellious Slaves" dated 2nd January 1832. Source: Public Records Office, London, CO 137/181, as shown on www.slaveimages.org. Sponsored by the Virginia Foundation for the Humanities and the University of Virginia Library. Courtesy of authors Jerome S. Handler and Michael L. Tuite Jr.

However, they have ordered us to cut the cane on a day that is undeniably ours," he repeated.

"Will we cut the ripening cane stalks during our holiday without pay?" he demanded again.

"No, no, no, we will not. The cane will rot in the cane pieces," they bawled.

"Go forth and make merry. You must talk to our brothers and sisters about the burden, the planters have placed on all of us in our own time," he urged.

"Peacefully and very determinedly, together we must stand steadfastly against their continued tyranny," he told them.

They scattered to plantations across the island, to family and friends that they had not seen during the year, to celebrate their three dearly loved days. As they partied, they talked about the further yoke the planters had put upon them. Their families, friends and colleagues, were enraged by the planters' demands on their treasured days. The talking drums had also spread the dilemma placed on them by the planters. The drums helped to organise their discontent and frustration.

All of a sudden, fires raged on plantations near and far. The trash house on Kensington Estate burst into flames, as well as Kensington great house itself, followed by many other estate houses. The island was a brightly lit beacon. The cane pieces and their buildings were on fire the length and breadth of the island. My brothers and sisters across the island had had enough of the planters' arrogance and greed. They linked the demands of the slave owners, with the rumours of the ending of their enslavement. The clandestine and circulating whispers had talked about the freedom papers that had been granted to them by the King of England. The Backra had burnt them. They would burn the Backras' cane pieces and free instead themselves.

The agents, overseers and militia, rushed to put out the burning buildings. The furious Africans relit them again and again. The army fired on them with their muskets; they disarmed them and battered them to death. The enslaved Africans were taking their freedom. They took their island, and for eight days it was theirs. The planters offered them bribes to return to their plantations, they employed their usual tricks. They had tried to set them against each other, but the enslaved Africans had learnt that important lesson. They could not divide them this time. Determinedly, they stood together against the ruthless planters, their government and their army. The slave masters fled and barricaded themselves in their plantation buildings. They summoned reinforcements to end the uprising. My courageous brothers and sisters on the plantations had hidden and protected their young leader Deacon Sam Sharpe, from the planters, the Maroons and the army, to guarantee their emancipation.

Viciously, the planters' army suppressed the uprising when they arrived. Ferociously, my family members were slaughtered like animals. The remainder lived only because the planters could not destroy all their property. They could not get rid of those, who would produce the next generation of slaves to work in their cane pieces without pay.

The British army had searched the island for many, many more months before they found our brave and fearless leader, Deacon Sharpe. They made many speeches, about the importance of obedience and respect for the earthly order. They informed the Africans that the Lord God in his great wisdom had made them the masters and the Negroes the slaves to work on their plantations. They must accept this arrangement or live with the consequences. Next, they hung him, along with three hundred and fifty Africans in the town's square. It was their revenge and warning, to those on their plantations planning further resistance to them. Thousands of enslaved Africans had died to end slavery. The island returned to their control.

The Christmas uprising had traumatised and shocked the planters and their Parliament in England. Swiftly, they acted in great haste to salvage their future. The events in the African controlled island of St Domingue, as well as the independent Spanish colonies of Gran Colombia, on the mainland, haunted their sleeping and waking hours.

CHAPTER 19

The planters fight back

The governor agreed with the dejected planters that the violent Christmas uprising, which began on the island just after Christmas in 1831 and which had lasted eight days, could not be allowed to happen again. It had taken the army and government, many months to bring the plantations and the island back under their control. The rebellion was a total shock to everyone; they had not expected it. However, the Parliament in England had dealt quickly and decisively with the insurgency, they must follow their lead. Their slaves had almost driven them from their island.

He hinted that the Western rebellion was probably encouraged and financed by the Negro Republic in St Domingue, now renamed Haiti by the Negro generals. He had also heard rumours, that the Baptist preachers had also encouraged their slaves, to rise up and burn their plantations. The British government would deal with the Baptists preachers in due course.

He also informed them that the insurrection was led by a Negro Deacon of the Baptist faith. They had many, many more enemies. The Negro generals in St Domingue and their allies in Gran Colombia on the mainland would try again and again, to dislodge them from their island. The British government he told them had allowed Simon Bolivar to stay on their island when the Spanish government had attempted to kill him because he plotted to overthrow them. He then used his stay on their island, to plot and drive the Spanish King and government from many of their colonies on the South American mainland.

Now, this very ungrateful person had been over the years, scheming with the Negro President in Haiti, to drive them from their islands, he believed. They must learn these lessons and take bold action to maintain control of their islands and their slaves.

Gradually, his rage subsided, then he addressed his audience solemnly.

"We have come together to mourn the loss of many of our most prominent families, our family members and friends that were slaughtered by the Negro savages. They were slain, during the time that they were in control of our island. We are still seeking the bodies of all our loved ones. The Army will continue to look for them so we can give them the Christian burial they deserve. Our plantations are in ruins; our homes and buildings have also been wrecked. It will cost thousands and thousands of guineas to make them profitable again. The government will not pay, the money lenders are reluctant to lend money to repair our plantations because they fear more insurrections from our slaves," he sighed.

"Neither will the King pay for any more troops to be sent to the island. He has other priorities for the money in the treasury. He demands a solution that will maintain his power, as well as the plantations intact for ever more. Alas, the tide has turned against slavery at home," he groaned.

"We should have known that the abolitionists would not be satisfied with ending the slave trade. Now, they have worked relentlessly to end slavery on our plantations too. They have succeeded entirely. Olaudah Equiano, Ignatius Sancho, Ottobah Cugoano and many ex-slaves in England had campaigned for the ending of the slave trade along with slavery. Now, they have brought about the changes they had worked tirelessly to achieve. Indeed, Sirs the Abolitionist have also used the recent violent uprising at Christmas, on this island to their advantage. Vigorously, they have highlighted the destruction of the plantations and also the cost of repairing them. Recently, they have also enlisted the help of an ex-slave woman, called Mary Prince from the island of Antigua. She talked about her and her fellow slaves' experience of slavery. Her revelations have injured 'our cause' considerably and enhanced the Abolitionist demands for the ending of slavery. Mary Prince, Olaudah and many other Blackies in England, have had a tremendous impact on the workers in the North of England too," he admitted.

"Passionately, the Negro woman spoke to these white workers, they sympathised with her demand for the ending of slavery. They identified with the slaves' condition because of their working conditions in the factories, mills and mines in the Northern industries. They understood the Negroes' struggles to free themselves, because of their long and extremely hazardous working conditions, as well as their pitiful wages. Many of them call themselves, 'white slaves' in the factories, mines and mills of their homeland. Many appreciate the fact that they still have their families close by and that they still lived in the country of their birth. Many of them actively support the Anti-slavery coalition. This coalition had forcefully made the case for the abolition of slavery in Parliament. It would only get worse. We have to adapt to the changing situation we find ourselves in and make the necessary adjustments swiftly," he advised them calmly.

Wearily, he told them.

"We must learn from the Spanish and French experience. We must not allow our slaves to drive us from these prized and profitable islands. The government had voted to make the necessary adjustments, we must do the same. We must secure our own interests and the interest of our King and country, whatever it takes without delay," he counselled them.

Optimistically, he continued.

"At home the focus was now on the industries in the North of England. The plantations were often distant memories for the majority of owners, many of whom had never visited their plantations in the islands or on the mainland. Their plantations had been profitable investments. They now took second place to the developing business and commercial interests of the country. Individuals with money from their overseas plantations had and were now investing in the new factories and businesses opportunities available to make even more money," he informed them.

"This was the way forward, this was the way to go," he recommended.

He introduced them to an overbearing money lender from England.

"Look here," he said. "We have among us one of the very enterprising gentlemen from the profitable East India Company. This company had financed many business enterprises and industries in the past. I'm sure he will tell us more about the new and profitable business opportunities, that are developing in the industrial North of our fatherland," he said warmly and graciously.

Turning to an ashen–faced young man, the governor, asked him to tell the gathering about the British East India Company. The company had colonised and grabbed land in that country too. The company was importing cotton from India, the Far East and nearer home in the Southern states of North America, to revive the cloth making industries in the North of England.

"Yes, pray tell us more about these promising developments," begged the snivelling planters.

"I can assure you all that investing in the factories and mines, will give you greater returns on your money. The profits will be much more than you ever got from your plantations with slave labour," said the ashen–faced young man rubbing his hands to emphasise the money to be made.

He continued.

"The cities of Manchester, Sheffield and Birmingham as well as the surrounding towns and villages are filled with cheap labour. People are leaving the land for this new form of employment. Factories can guarantee these workers employment throughout the year, unlike working on their farms with its droughts and prices that rise and fall yearly. We should be pleased because their massive numbers drive down wages. Many factory owners are paying their workers a fraction of a shilling for working between twelve and eighteen hours each day. They prefer children and young women because they are much cheaper than men. I know of masters, who employ children aged seven years and younger, to fetch and carry for the adult workers, which speeds up production. Their small hands and bodies can go betwixt and under the machine parts pulling out fastened thread and cloth. Gladly, their parents will accept anything for them," he told them.

"Another enterprising gentleman, I have been told gathered bands of nimble-fingered children. These children picked the pockets of gentle folk for their master, for a bed on the floor of his rough and ready home. They got a bowl of watery soup after a very long day in the streets. This was a lot more than their parents could give them. Then there are the small children, whose flexible limbs can bend and twist to go up factory chimneys to sweep them. They get paid less than a half-penny a day if they are very lucky," he grinned.

"Others, happily go down the mines for more than twelve hours a day. Their employers are growing rich from their work, even though they have to pay them a very, very small wage. Many, many parents, as well as the workhouses, will gladly give you their children. They will ask nothing for them, except that you house, clothe and feed them until they are sixteen years old. Think of the free labour you will have. They are called apprentices," he beamed.

"Then, there are the massive profits to be reaped in the future, from the continuing developments of the railways in Britain. If you invest now, think of the profit you will make in the long term," he advised them.

He pinched his fingers together to show the small wage they would be paying their future workers and opened his palms to indicate the enormous returns on their investments.

"I promise you that soon there will be machines to do the work in the factories. Then you will not have to pay any wages at all. Thus making even more profit for yourselves, after you have paid for the machines," the Banker told them convincingly.

"So I beseech you all to come and join us in this great enterprise, to make 'The British Empire' even more powerful than it is today," coaxed the ashen-faced young man.

He continued gleefully and rubbed his palms together over and over again to show his excitement at what he was about to reveal. He lowered his voice and told them.

"Some of you will have plenty of money to invest very soon. The abolitionists have succeeded in stopping the transportation of slaves in British ships. Now, they have campaigned for the ending of slavery on your plantations. The coalition is supported by the Wesley's' from their pulpit and the fanatical Mr Clarkson. I believe Mr Wilberforce is the spoke person for the campaign in Parliament that is seeking to end slavery on your plantations," he warned them.

"Everyone in England knows that the plantations are a hotbed of rebellion. The Western insurrection has traumatised all of us, we must act decisively. The constant revolts by the slaves, disrupt the production of sugar and rum. This has had catastrophic consequences on the incomes and profit from the plantations. It cannot continue. We must find ways of making the estates run more smoothly and efficiently for our benefit. We must adjust I say, we must change and quickly too. The Negroes have their talking drums. They know what is going on in and outside the island. It will be more difficult in the coming years, to maintain the level of order and production, that you have struggled over the years to uphold. Plantation slavery is dying. We can choose to ignore the signs, or take control of this situation. We cannot allow the abolitionists and our slaves to make the decision for us," he told them grimly.

He continued in a very matter of a fact way.

"The plantations are proving to be a hazard for all of you right now. However, you can count on your government, they will never abandon you, their loyal subjects. They will not desert these prized sugar islands, that have given them wealth as well as making them the rulers of the world. They will not forsake you and your plantations because our competitors in

Europe are eagerly waiting to snatch them from us. They want to reap the great wealth, we have enjoyed from growing sugar, for over one hundred and seventy-five years," he informed them.

"I know," he continued, "the abolition of slavery is being negotiated as we gather here. I can assure you that if slavery is brought to an end, your slaves will not be freed overnight. There will be time, for both masters and slaves to adjust to the new situation. How can our Negroes be expected to look after themselves? We have to prepare them for freedom, to live responsible lives, serve the Lord and continue to respect and obey us as their masters. They are merely children, young children that need to be taught and trained to be industrious. They must be made to accept our ways of thinking and doing things; they must continue to work for our benefit first and foremost. A transition is necessary, 'apprenticeships' they call it. It allows your slaves to learn about our much-admired and democratic traditions of justice, equality and freedom. It is also a breathing space for you to make the necessary changes, that will not hurt your pockets. Surely, it will be foolish to destroy yourselves and your plantations at one stroke, by giving them their total freedom," he confided in them.

"The ending of slavery will be managed, I promise you. Your interests and that of our country will be Parliament's first priority, I guarantee you. They will give you compensation as well as sufficient time to adapt to this new situation when the Act is passed," reassured the ashen-faced young man.

"You will get compensation for every Negro you free. I believe it is between thirty and a hundred guineas for each slave, depending on their age and physical condition. These generous payments will give you the money to invest in the factories, mines, mills and railways as they develop. There is a bonus too: you will be able to keep your plantations. Your field slaves will continue to work on your estates for six years after the abolition is announced, for food and lodgings only," chuckled the ashen-faced young man.

The new British Administrative Building in Spanish Town, Jamaica.

A sigh of relief filled the room. The planters began to alter their thinking. They would no longer curse and despise their Parliament, for first abolishing the carrying of slaves in British ships and now the ending of slavery on their plantations. Maybe, they thought there was money to be made by ending slavery in its current form.

The ashen-faced young man concluded the meeting by reminding the planters, that they had nothing to lose by ending slavery in its present form. They were indeed lucky that the ending of slavery would give them two sources of income. The compensation for their slaves would give them money to invest in Britain. They would also keep their plantations as well as their field slaves, to work for them as apprentices for six more long years.

The banker had summed up the future accurately. The Western uprising of December 1831-32 had alarmed the planters and their government. Violent slave uprisings in Antigua, the Bahamas, Cuba, Martinique, Tortola, St John and the Southern states of North America had panicked them too. These ferocious uprisings had focussed the minds of the colonial governments and their administration. The British Government decided to take charge and manage the threat to their empire and wealth.

On the 28th August 1833, the Act for the Abolition of Slavery in the islands and the mainland of South America, Canada, Cape Colony in South Africa and Mauritius was passed. The Act promised to compensate the planters to free some categories of enslaved Africans, within specified periods of time. It allowed for the field slaves, to continue working for the plantation owners for another six years for food and lodgings only. A year later on 1st August 1834, the terms of the 1833 Act was implemented. Officially, the enslaved Africans were free. However, the Act had continued their enslavement as Apprentices.

The enslaved Africans had prepared mentally and physically for their freedom over the centuries. They had fought continuously to end their subjugation. However, the planters and their government had crushed their aspirations at a stroke. Suddenly, they had become apprenticed labourers. They were now being given the opportunity, to learn how to work on the plantations and acquire ways of thinking and behaving, that were alien to them. These behaviours would only serve the interests of those who had enslaved them and who would continue to do so in the future.

The enslaved Africans would continue to work for up to forty-five hours a week on the plantations under the same harsh regimes as before. The rest of their time was theirs, to use wisely to earn money to buy back their freedom from the apprenticeships. They had wrung their freedom from the planters but in keeping with their past practices the slave masters would use their victory against them. They would use it to continue their economic power and dominance over them. At the same time, the slave masters would receive generous compensation, for each enslaved African still working on their plantations, for no wages.

"The more it changes, the more it stays the same," I wailed.

CHAPTER 20

Frustration

The enslaved Africans had been passionately and diligently fighting for their liberation, from the inception of their enslavement. Their rebellion of 1831-32 had ensured a swift response from the British government. Brutally, they had put down their rebellion because they feared their determination to liberate themselves. However, instead of freeing them as the 1833 Act of Abolition stated, it had re-enslaved the majority of them for a further six years.

Religiously, the planters and their accomplices prepared to celebrate the birth of their god at this time. They were eager to thank him for giving them the opportunity, to re-enslave the Africans on their plantations to maintain their wealth and power. The Africans had planned to incorporate their three days of Christmas revelry into their freedom festivities and celebrations. But once again their yearning for freedom had been snatched from them. Their Christmas festivities were scarred, by the criminal behaviour of the British Parliament.

The enslaved Africans prepared for Christmas too. They began by using the bits and pieces they had taken from the planters' stores. These were zero payment for their never-ending labour on their plantations as well as the theft of their total liberation. They used these scraps to make costumes and special masks for their very uplifting African performances at Christmas. Provisions were gathered from across the island, molasses, salted and dried fish as well as meat. Gladly, the tight-fisted planters gave them the liver, heart, kidneys, tails, heads and feet of the animals that they did not want. These made delicious dishes which graced their Christmas tables.

The compounds swelled with visitors from near and far. The yams, sweet potatoes, maize and cassava grown on their provision grounds pushed up through the earth, to be ready for the festivities. The banana and plantain trees bent with their weighty fruit while the coconut palms fanned the hot earth. The fruit trees did not disappoint, mangoes, guavas, naseberries, sweet and soursops were gathered from across the island for their merriment. The children were at the heart of the celebrations. They challenged each other.

"Let's see who can catch the biggest crab," Kofi dared his friends.

"You can catch crabs. I'm going to catch the biggest crayfish you've ever seen," Kwame promised. "I know where to find big ones," he grinned.

"I'll catch the biggest flying fish you'll ever set your eyes on," Abibi smiled.

"A juicy and nourishing sugarcane for the children who bring back the most fruits," promised the adults.

"Fruits and berries are coming up," they shrieked.

The medicine people brewed and stored mixtures to quench their thirst and keep away the spirits of those who had enslaved them. They didn't forget the offerings as well as paying respect to their ancestors. They had kept a watchful eye over them as best as they could. Meanwhile, they practiced the dances and rituals, they remembered or were taught by the elders. They thanked and paid tribute to the seasons, the fertile soil, the rain and sun for the abundance they had given them on their small rocky plots and provision grounds.

The Junkanoo bands paraded around the compounds. They alleviated, as best as they could, their disappointment as well as their fury at their prolonged enslavement. They drew everyone in, to fully take part in the high-spiritedness. They circled the gigantic trees several times and gathered children as they went. The bands chanted and sung in the half-forgotten languages of their audience. They invited the audience to join them. Generously, the revellers fed them to show their gratitude for the entertainment and unloading 'The Annual Junkanoo and Anancy Show' would give them.

The delicious smell of roasted fish, peanuts, sweet potatoes, corn and other foodstuff, rose from the glowing embers of the makeshift stoves and fires, reassuring the revellers of the night to come. The procession completed, they disappeared and returned taking their place on the stage, in front of a jubilant but seething audience.

Slowly, they moved apart. Instinctively, the Junkanoo players and I, Anancy, fell into the role of those who had extended their enslavement. Together, we would allow them to rip apart the planters and their government, for a short time relieving their pain and disappointment for the evening. The show began.

A pale face and wizened planter, as well as his freckled face wife and child in rags, gaped at the audience. They seemed not to have eaten for days, they begged for food. Contemptuously, the generous Africans threw their scraps at them. They watched in delight as they scrambled for them. The planter pushed his wife and child over. He grabbed the scraps and forced them into his mouth. The planter's wife and child held out their hands and begged for food.

"Shame on you, shame on you," they cried.

"Lazy, lazy, useless creatures," they repeated.

"A couple of days without us and you have become brutal towards your own family members. Look at what you have become without us to slave for you. Hungry, thin, smelly, greedy, dirty, depraved and worthless," they howled and bellowed.

"What about the drunks and gluttons are we going to mock them tonight?" they asked.

Instantly, three bloated and drunken crimson-faced planters wobbled onto the stage. They lolled about stinking of rum. They fell over each time, as they fought to get to the cask of rum. An enraged African ran over to them and pushed them around and around the stage. The audience screamed in delight. They held out their goblets and begged for more rum.

"Pour it over them, drown them in the commodity that they have used to enslave and re-enslave us," they screeched.

"These are the planters that have stolen our labour. They have exploited us every day of our lives for three centuries and more," they bawled.

"These are the slave masters that have fastened us, to their cane pieces for another six long years," they wailed.

"What shall we do with them?" they roared.

"Drown them, drown them, drown them," they insisted.

"Push down and hold their heads, in the commodity that they have used to enslave us until they expire," they ordered.

The planters twisted and struggled to free themselves, but the infuriated Africans held them. They demanded they beg for mercy. The plantation owners resisted and sneered.

"You are our Negro slaves, we do not and will not beg our Blackies for mercy," they flung at the furious Africans.

The incensed Africans plunged their heads into casks of rum until they saw the blue of death on their faces. Then, the drunkards pleaded for their compassion and their lives. They chucked them onto the floor, and they gasped for air. The audience rolled them into a nearby gully.

Next, the enraged audience demanded the overseers.

"Let's see the overseer's whip," they hollered in unison.

As requested, a wrinkled and pasty face overseer fell in front of the audience.

"What shall we do with him?" they chanted.

"Whip him, whip him," they screamed.

At the sight of the whip the overseer fell on his knees, he curled himself up into the smallest of figures and begged for mercy.

"Look here," he said, "my delicate white body could not withstand the lash of the cow's whip. I'll give you anything, anything, if you spare me the whip," pleaded the pathetic overseer.

The angry Africans laughed and laughed their most scornful laugh. The cow's whip that he had used daily in the cane piece on them whizzed above his head and close to his face terrifying him. They demanded over and over again, "Whip him, whip him, whip him."

They screamed until they were hoarse.

"I've fifty guineas in my little house, you can have it if you spare me the cow's whip," sobbed the overseer appealing to the humanity of his persecutors.

"Only fifty guineas they bawled, our lives and freedom are worth more than fifty guineas," they informed him.

"That's all I have," he moaned.

"Find more if you want your life," they hissed.

"Maybe, I have a little more in my modest house," he said trembling.

"Let the yellow belly coward go for a hundred guineas. It will buy the freedom of some of our elders, so they can live out the rest of their lives as free human beings," they insisted.

"Anything, anything," pleaded the cringing and cowering overseer.

They shoved him into the gully with the drunkards.

"Bring on the 'wigs' and 'gowns' of the Great British Parliament," they screamed.

"Let us see those cold-hearted brutes that have lengthened our enslavement. They have destroyed our hunger for freedom," they wailed and sobbed.

The white wigs and black gowns representing the Parliament that had stabbed them in the back accordingly appeared on the stage in front of the vexed Africans. They threw objects into the air and struck and punctured the 'wigs' and 'gowns'. They surged forward to rip apart the wigs and gowns to shreds. They raged and screamed, at the representations, of those that had snatched their goal of total liberation and autonomy.

The wigs and gowns floated out of their reach into the spreading branches of the Guango tree, just like the freedom that they had fought for over the centuries and which now eluded them. They could not be pacified. They wanted more time to vent their wrath on the planters and their paid accomplices, who had persecuted and exploited them daily over the centuries. They loathed the deceit and cruelty of the plantation owners and their government, along with the continued theft of their labour. They would have to wait for another time, to unleash their collective rage and scorn on their oppressors.

Noisily, the audience cheered and whistled. The crowd cheered me as well as the Junkanoo players for the temporary release we had given them. They hugged and lifted us into the air.

"Three cheers for Anancy and the Junkanoo players," they screamed.

Generously, they offered us casks of rum, a dozen chickens and three sacks of guinea corn each.

"Thank you, thank you, we all said," touched by the unselfishness of the audience.

Acutely, we felt their appreciation for the temporary release we had given them. Unexpectedly, a reveller ran into the open space and quivered and shuddered in an uncontrolled way. The young woman spoke to everyone, not in the Creole they used every day in the cane pieces, but in a tongue most of them did not know or had forgotten long ago. Slowly, her limbs became quiet; she buckled and sunk lifelessly onto the earth. The ancient African men and women among the audience nodded approvingly as the power of the ancestors' spirit moved among everyone composing, strengthening and preparing them for the battles ahead. The African religious revival had begun. The struggle for their total liberation had started.

The Abeng horns along with the rhythm of the African drums welcomed the dawn. They reminded each and everyone that they were still on the plantations, even though they and their kinfolk had fought hard for them to be free. Their brothers and sisters, on the islands of St Kitts, Trinidad and West Coast Demerara on the mainland, expressed the feelings that were felt by all of them. Violently, they responded to the content of the Act. They burnt and refused to work on the plantations until the decision was reversed. Collectively, the Africans across the enslaved world challenged the Act, which purported to give them their freedom, but at the same time re-enslaved them as apprentices.

The drums and horns also announced the end of the festivities across the island's sprawling plantations. They warned of the battles ahead. The status of the enslaved Africans had changed from slaves to apprentices for another six long years, but their condition was still the same. They were still bound to the cane pieces. They would have to work for up to forty-five hours a week, for food and lodgings only. They continued to sleep in the same grubby huts allocated to them and their families. They ate meals that were barely enough, to satisfy their rumbling bellies and provide the nutrients to work semi-naked in the cane pieces.

Undeniably, they had achieved the physical freedom they had fought for over the centuries. However, it had been viciously snatched from them. In the future, their unrestricted freedom and total emancipation were their unconditional goal, within the shortest possible time. It wasn't far off.

CHAPTER 21

A fraudulent freedom

The freed Africans rose with the rising sun to mark the dawn of this new and momentous day. This extraordinary day that would continue to shape their quest for total freedom and self-direction. Across the islands and the mainland, the conditionally freed Africans climbed to the highest points, to ensure that they would see the birth of this historic day. This victorious day that would transform their status from slaves to free Africans. August 1st, 1834, marked another chapter in their hard-fought victory over the slave masters, putting them on the road to dignity and self-fulfilment, for each and every one.

The island's capital in Spanish Town, with its red brick government buildings, buzzed with excitement and anticipation on this incredible day. The roof tops, trees, as well as the distant hilly landscape, heaved under the weight of the liberated revellers. Ladies decked in their finest garments and trinkets, men in their most colourful breeches and starched collars. Children in their best, hung onto the breeches, waistcoats, petticoats and dress tails of the adults, craving a view of this emerging and remarkable day.

I washed and oiled my hairy body. I wore my black and white top and tails, at this very eventful juncture. I made my web high in the uppermost branches of a Guango tree, to observe and take part in the celebrations. I marvelled at the resilience of my brothers and sisters, who had wrenched their freedom from the planters. They had been betrayed, but their joyfulness had no boundaries. Their jubilation on this day temporarily banished their grief at their continued enslavement.

The elevated and multi-coloured Junkanoo bands dressed in purple and adorned with animal masks and shells, as well as playing the horns and drums, led the joyful revellers and their collective aspirations for the future. This glorious day was so precious, and it promised so much, they all needed to witness its dawn.

"We must value and cherish this extraordinary day. Today is a testimony to our strength and determination as the sons and daughters of our motherland. We have ended slavery, the victory is ours," I said dangling from above in my poker dot bow tie to the amusement of my fellow revellers.

Then, he moved towards the makeshift podium. Carefully, he placed his six-foot frame and bulk onto the stand. The ecstatic Africans encircled him. He took a deep breath, mulling over what he was going to say. A button popped on his tight fitting white shirt, it revealed jet black skin crossed by raised ridges from the overseer's whip. His raised ridges replicated under the garment of his audience.

"Today, today," he repeated after another pause, "is our day." "A magnificent day, a day we have fought long and hard for. We must observe it in whatever way we chose collectively and individually, even though it falls very short of what we have struggled and fought for over the centuries."

He continued.

"Respect for our ancestors and the courage and strength they have instilled in us, to enable us to bring about this exceptional accomplishment today."

He poured spirit on the ground and then paid tribute to their ancestral home in Africa.

"To our ancestors who have served us well in our daily affliction."

"To our motherland, that nourished us in her womb until we were ripped from her."

"To the African soil that fed and sustained us, as well as the sun, the moon and stars that gave us warmth, light and life."

"To the precious rain that bathed us and gave us growth and abundance."

"To our extended families who grieve at our separation and our longing to be together once again."

The libation ended and once again he addressed his conscientious listeners.

"We know," he said, "the task ahead of us, the form has changed, but the substance is still the same. We go forward into a fraudulent future. We must take for ourselves and our family members as much as we can wrench from the iron fists of the slave masters and their gang of tyrants, as we did in the past. Our future will have to be wrestled from the hands of the Backra and their government during the so-called apprenticeships. It is slavery, slavery disguised in its worst form. The day is young and the night is even younger, to our collective future."

Once more he poured spirit onto the parched dry earth. Instantaneously, the earth swallowed it. Curtsying respectfully to this leader among them, the crowd dispersed to all corners of the island to celebrate. Food, drink, music dance and their religious rituals filled the days and night ahead. The African revival and resistance had reached its zenith.

Part Two

INTRODUCTION

'An African Journey', Part Two tells the story of the Africans' determination to overcome the major obstacles, placed in their way after 1834, by the British Parliament. Having learnt first-hand of the despicable means the planters employed to continue their enslavement, they sought secure ways of liberating themselves for all time.

They drew on, the ancient organisational and financial practices of their motherland, to end the planters' tyranny over them. Some continued to flee the plantations to retake their independence. Many worked very hard on their miniature house plots and provision grounds away from the plantations. They used the proceeds to buy their freedom; thus guaranteeing the demise of the plantation system and, therefore, slavery.

They fled from the plantations and became the people they were born to and wanted to be. Naturally, they returned to the knowledge buried deep within their souls, which slavery had solidified into their being. Plantation slavery had enhanced their profound respect and reverence for the land and all that it brought forth. They craved the land. They became one with the only source the soil that could satisfy their longing for self-sufficiency, autonomy, independence and human dignity. They discarded the commodity which had distorted production in the islands and the mainland. Naturally, they flaunted the rich and natural culture of their motherland, half-forgotten maybe, but cherished along with the memories of a distant homeland secretly simmering in their souls. Unapologetically, they sang, danced and celebrated joyfully as they moved onto the open hillsides, marginal lands and gullies of the islands and the mainland.

They fixed their African heritage and humanity, into the fabric of these marginal lands, tarnished by commodity slavery. They rejected the restraints which sugar cultivation had imposed on them. They used the resilience that had won them their freedom, to carve out for themselves and their descendants a stable and dignified future as Africans and versatile human beings.

CHAPTER 1

Kufuo Amoah

Intermittently, rain fell on Akin's scrubland. The scrubland provided just enough grazing for the village's herds of goats and a few lean cows. Diligently, the young shepherds cared for their valuable and prized herds. Sometimes, they wandered to the edge of the village, to carry out their duties. Taking refuge under the shade of a thorny shrub the shepherds shared the midday meal that would keep them, until a meal at dusk. They stroked the elongated faces and smooth skins of their stunning creatures, asking for a morsel from their meagre meal. The daily ritual of stroking and grooming these beautiful creatures bound them together. This ensured they knew every detail and whim of the herd, which might need their prompt attention. The shepherds' lean and striking animals led them further afield in search of food.

All of a sudden, birds screeched and flew out of the wiry trees. The shepherds turned and herded their goats away from the impending danger. The herd bolted, as the loin-clothed raiders rushed towards the young shepherds.

"Run Kufuo, run, they are not after our goats, this time, they are after us. They want to seize and sell us to the slave galleons that frequently dock at Elmina Fort," Osei shrieked in terror.

The boys ran as fast as they could unable to choose their path, their bare feet landed on thorns that slowed their retreat. The net and club-wielding thieves encircled them. A shepherd got away, as he had wandered away from the animals and was out of sight. The vile creatures enclosed the small lean bodies of the boy shepherds with their nets. They plotted their route to avoid the wrath of Akin's population, as well as the families of these young and dutiful shepherds.

The animals encircled them pulling at the nets in vain, to free their young in pain. They bleated and whimpered in tenderness. Lifting his hand, Kufuo stroked the beautiful creatures in front of him, as their sorrowful eyes met. Kufuo felt the smooth, delicate lick and smell of the herd on his face. Lifting the net after the hands of the boys were bound together, the furtive thieves skirted the village of Akin and set out towards Cape Coast and Elmina Fort.

The boy shepherds tumbled over the thick terrain, their feet swollen and punctured by the thorny scrubland. Their bodies ached and bled as the captors' whip tore into their bare flesh. It opened half healed lacerations and made new raw gashes, on their once healthy and flawless Ebony skins. Their bodies throbbed with pain, blood oozed from their wounds, but they had to go on. Now and again, their pace slowed. However, the shock of the metal spikes thrust into their delicate young flesh, forced them to move faster, pain overwhelmed their throbbing bodies and senses. They stumbled and staggered, their feet became weaker and weaker as their blood drained from their festering wounds. They tripped, lurched forwards and flopped over; their chins almost touched the brambles that stung their blistered feet. Nevertheless, they went on, and on, they only rested when the thieves were too tired to go on. The spineless thieves hid during the day and trudged through moonless nights to the coast.

They entered Cape Coast at night. The whiteness of the whitewashed fort was cloaked in darkness. The captives were thrown onto the fort's dilapidated basement floor. Their stiff and aching bodies sunk deep into the hard floor. It caressed their rotting wounds, for a moment they felt relieved. The boys dragged their tender and sore limbs together, closed their eyes and attempted to sleep forever.

Startled, they awoke as torrents of water struck their faces and bodies, it cooled their stiff and painful torso. Corn Stew and water were shovelled into their mouths. They choked and vomited their first solid food since their capture. The stench filled the basement. They looked around, feelings of humiliation flooded the space around them; their fellow captives stared intently into the distance, this was now their everyday routine and reality.

As darkness fell, the monotonous sound of the splashing waves onto the shore squeezed through the cracks and put them to sleep once again after they had eaten. The bustle and smell of this ancient seaport woke them for the second time. The morning sun rose, and multitudes of fishing vessels stirred up the sea as they sailed towards their fishing grounds or returned from their nightly fishing. The constant screeching of seabirds, as well as the chattering of human voices, comforted them during their stopover.

Day by day, hungrily they ate the captive meal of corn and fish stew, placed in their cells. They were thankful for regular meals. Sometimes, they were given pieces of fruit from the trees, that framed the coastline. They knew they were being fattened for an imminent journey. Their minds were full of torture and pain, as their families, as well as their animals, preoccupied their waking and sleeping hours. Their bodies were becoming stronger as the days and nights passed. At night, they were in Akin by the compound fires preparing for the day to come. They were playing games or casually talking with family as well as friends, to pass the hours before bedtime. They longed to return to those familiar everyday amusements.

One night, a matronly woman came to them and took them gently to the seashore. She watched them bathe with their hands still tied together. The boys looked at each other, they were afraid to acknowledge that this was probably their last time together. The teenagers had given each other hope and companionship, throughout their gruelling trek and stay on the hard basement floor. They huddled together and tried to recall and share pieces of their past life as dutiful shepherds and captives. The prospect of their imminent separation overwhelmed and terrified them.

They had been one throughout their capture and imprisonment on the fort's compacted floor.

The matron grabbed their arms roughly, she pulled them out of the water, but her soft and gentle eyes told them she was not responsible for their plight. Tenderly, she massaged their bodies with perfumed oils. Carefully, she scrutinised every inch of their flesh for cuts and infestations. Satisfied, she gave them pieces of stick to chew to clean their teeth. The youths sucked the potent juices that would further strengthen them. She returned them to the fort, but not into the room they had shared, but to the lowest floor and untied them. The matron led them to the doorways of the basement hovels.

Their premonition had come true. They were being separated from each other, their families and their motherland forever. They reached out to each other, their fingertips touched as they were shoved into the two separate underground hovels. African bodies, children, women and men filled them. These demoralised and ailing captives were about to be violently shipped across the Atlantic Ocean away from Africa's shore to another far off continent under duress. Kufuo could not count the bodies that filled the huge underground hovel. Definitively, the door slammed shut behind them. He yearned for Osei. Briefly, his features appeared before him, but he could not speak to him. Angrily, he turned and saw the carved wooden door, which opened onto the pier. The galleons were awaiting their cargo.

That night terrified screams and dreams of Akin disrupted their sleep. The battered and robust oak door at the far end of their prison creaked open; the smell of the familiar fishy sea filled his nostrils. Distressed, he looked ahead and saw the white sails of a white washed galleon with its white crew. Some Africans were loading and unloading casks and other goods onto it. His body froze. He was about to leave Africa, the continent that had reared him. The boy shepherd was leaving behind his beloved animals, which had filled his life with purpose and fulfilment. They were all leaving behind their mothers, fathers, siblings, cousins, and extended families, who were being ripped

An impression of Elmina Fort, Cape Coast, Ghana, slave warehouse.

from them forever. Fear seized them. That night, they dreamt over and over again of their escape and return to their villages.

Their feet were rooted to the floor. Nevertheless, the bodies behind them pushed them in the direction of the enormous engraved solid oak door towards the galleon. Once on board, the captives were forced into the hold of the vessel. Reluctantly, they shuffled towards the berthed rows and planks that filled its hold. Bodies were squeezed onto the rows until each one was filled and seated they were bound together, with iron handcuffs to stop them from jumping overboard. The sequence was repeated again and again until all the planks were filled. Hopelessly, they slumped and sprawled with fatigue and sleep, on top of each other. Their imposed closeness comforted them. Dignified but distressed, this vast human cargo compressed into the miniature holds of galleons, existed, breathed and shared each other's life, air, pain, excretion, resistance and frequent death.

Daily, raw and whiffy men with bright red faces stuffed corn stew followed by water into their mouths; at intervals, they threw water over their festering and failing bodies to renew them. The captives did not know that these people and faces existed in their homelands or on the earth. The solid carved oak door slammed shut. The luxury of the hard floor in the fort, as well as their motherland, was lost to them forever.

Now and again, they became aware of the rocking of their floating prison in choppy seas and the constant sting of the guards' whips on their tender flesh. The whip stung their limbs and their senses, pain engulfed them, and a shroud covered their existence. If they managed to survive or chose to finish this horrendous journey, dazed they stumbled off the galleons. They staggered onto a small clear coastline, framed by coconut trees similar to the ones they left months before.

Once again, the prisoners were scrutinised by foul smelling red-faced men dressed in shiny tight clinging coloured clothes, which ended halfway up their legs. Their upper bodies were covered with bright cloth, as well as an outer garment over the inner pieces. The buyers scrutinised the noblest Africans that had survived the most horrific journey, away from their blessed motherland, their relatives as well as their animals. They were poked and prodded with sticks. Red-hot branding irons sunk into their tender sun-starved flesh. Once again, pain rocked their senses, as well as their weak and frail bodies. They guessed that these creatures were their latest persecutors. Only death could take them back, to the routines, pleasures and familiarity of their homeland and family life.

Kufuo had felt very alone in the hold of the slave ship, with five hundred or more of his brothers and sisters around him. Osei had been taken from him; his animals, his family and his homeland had all been wrenched from him. He longed for his fellow shepherds and animals; they preoccupied his sleeping and waking hours. He wished Osei was chained to him their enforced closeness would comfort them both.

The resilient survivors propped each other up on the pure shimmering white sand. They stared inquisitively, at the lush green hilly and mountainous landscape all around them. They longed to be part of their welcoming and natural surroundings. One by one, the men were dragged to a makeshift platform, the women and children waited in terror. The slave trader mounted the platform. The sturdy males were marched before the agents and overseers. They inspected, jabbed and dug into their flesh.

They prised open and poked into their most intimate parts, to ensure that the goods were healthy. The wrangle for the human cargo began. Indifferently, Africans were sold and despatched to their plantations.

Kufuo's face erupted into a silent and broad grin of surprise and delight, as the tall, lanky limbs of Osei was thrown in front of the rickety platform. He was about to be sold; they had sailed in the hold of the same galleon, apart and in misery. Kufuo rejoiced inwardly. Roughly, the slave trader pulled Kufuo forward and pushed him onto Osei. Their enforced closeness comforted them as they stared at each other and became one again. Silently, they felt and savoured the joy of their reunion.

The slave trader promised the planters' overseers and agents, the best bargain they would ever get from him. They had been good customers over the years. Now that there were rumours about an act of abolition, it would soon curtail his secret trading. The Dutch man would have to find new markets for his abundant human cargo. He consoled himself that he would have to supply the remaining Spanish colonies because there was no talk of ending the slave trade or plantation slavery. The slave trader bemoaned the fact that the competition with the other European slave traders would further force down prices and, therefore, his profits. He would have to pack more Negroes from across the continent, in the hold of his galleon to maintain his earnings.

"Zees boys are easily worth two hundred guineas each," he said in his Dutch English accent.

"Zere is twenty good years' labour in zem. Zees bee the last good-looking boys I'll let ye have. By the time I return with another cargo in a couple of years, it will be impossible for me to sell any of my Negroes on this island and all zere other islands.

"My poor profits," he lamented.

"Give me 250 guineas for zem both," he pleaded.

The agent approached, he placed 200 guineas on the rickety platform. The slave trader grabbed it and stuffed it into his waistcoat. The agent had smiled and smiled, as he inspected their exquisite black skins and the sturdy bones buried beneath. The employee had asked to see their teeth and again he had grinned and grinned. He had made his final purchase his master would be pleased. These two would father many, many children. The boys would replace the ailing and worn out Negroes on the plantation. They would make fine workmen if and when the act abolishing slavery was passed.

Kufuo and Osei were loaded onto a cart by an ancient African. The boys could not speak to him, in silence he took them to a hut at Bax Hall plantation. They were glad to see a sea of African faces all around them, women and children as well as men. They opened their mouths to speak, but the stern gestures of the matrons forbade their speech. Instead, they heard words and phrases they did not know or understand. Words and speech they would be forced to learn rapidly as their back-breaking work in the cane pieces would begin within hours. They slept until the sun rose in the sky and announced the start of their gruelling working day in the cane piece.

CHAPTER 2

Kufuo's induction

Kufuo slept the sleep of death on his first night, as an enslaved boy, on the island. He woke abruptly as the noise of the bellowing bells forced the exhausted and still sleeping workers to rise. He followed the crowd, dressing, breakfasting, before trudging across the plantation yard towards the cane piece.

Mechanically, the heavy-eyed enslaved Africans entered the cane pieces. They dug, cut, weeded and chopped the cane, pushed along by the automated routine. Kufuo fell over and over, as the instinctive limbs of the experienced Africans worked continuously. He fell into the trenches and his mud-covered body alarmed his fellow workers. They worked steadily, with a watchful eye out for the overseer. He could not duplicate their methodical routine.

Regrettably, his tired eyes opened and closed with the lack of deep and restful sleep. The boy ambled among the cane rows for the morning until he fell asleep in a hidden corner of a field. In his dream, he saw the scrubland of Akin. He saw his flock grazing as well as pining for their lost shepherds. One by one, the elegant and elongated neck goats came forward and licked his face over and over again. Kufuo awoke and stroked their smooth, gleaming coat. The boy shepherd inhaled their scent along with the salty sea air. They urged him forward over the scrubland, his feet glided over the stiff scrub; they tingled on the well-known ground. Kufuo had returned to Akin. He ran with the flock over the scrubland like he had never done before.

The smell of the sea filled his whole self. Kufuo pulled up pieces of turf out of the hardened ground, the scent stung his nostrils. He crushed the bristles; their waning aroma caressed his face. Kufuo had the time of his life, with his herd and the other boy shepherds. They relived their past companionship. The animals led them to a secluded bathing hole, where they dived in guarded by their adoring animals. The boys swam to the depths and brought up tasty bits of sea plants, and these were speedily devoured by the herd licking their lips.

The herd skirted the town and ended up in their village just before nightfall. The shepherds placed their charges into cattle pens with bulky branches to chew their way to sleep. Kufuo wandered into the compound, the smell of dried fish stew caressed his taste buds. He washed his hands and took off his rough shepherd's clothes, before putting on his tunic for the evening. The women placed the evening meal of steaming cassava mash with fish stew in the centre of the circle; eagerly the men and boys had waited to consume it.

Impatiently, Kufuo awaited his turn to take a tasty morsel. It seemed like an eternity, but at last he scooped finger sized portions into his mouth and dribbled all over his tunic. He swallowed, his stomach waited excitedly for the next serving. His turn came over and over again until, finally, the empty bowls showed their enjoyment. The elders retired outdoors to take the local brew of fermented palm wine, while the youngsters moved to the open ground to rid themselves of the meal that had energised them. The women cleared up and ate in solitude.

The moon lit up the African scrubland, as the faint crash of waves on the seashore brought a calming breeze. It lulled their senses and prepared them for nightly tales and past times. One by one the boys told their much-loved stories. 'Anancy and the Goat Thieves' was their favourite. In the middle of the night, some goat thieves had led away three of the village's most prized animals. They hid them in a vast cave on the outskirts of the village. Then, they had returned to the village to resume their daily activities. The village elders demanded the return of the animals promptly. That night the missing goats entered the village. They began dancing and reciting to a crowd, bemused they stood around to be entertained. One by one, the goats came forward and gave their audience a riddle to solve. The thieves were terrified by the actions of the goats. They were frightened that their identities would soon be revealed, so they owned up to their crime. The thieves told the elders where they had hidden the goats and begged for their forgiveness.

The crowd gasped and shrieked, as one by one the goats in front of their eyes shrank into the tiniest of creatures, spiders. They crawled up a shiny silk thread into their spiral web anchored in a Nyala tree. Long live Anancy, the crowd chanted. Worn out by his day Kufuo slept peacefully.

CHAPTER 3

Kufuo's rude awakening

The sting of the overseer's whip cut deep into the sleeping body of the boy shepherd as he lay among the cane in the field. Startled, he jumped up, but again the whip lashed out at his body. He retreated into his smallest shape and dragged his burning limbs into the centre of the cane row. The whip followed his curled and retreating body, it hit out furiously at his robust but slender form. It continued to strike out at him as if it had a life of its own. His diminishing figure could not escape.

Blood seeped from the body of the boy shepherd and pain racked his sturdy but willowy shape. Suddenly, he felt moist and warm strokes caressing his body as the tongues of his herd licked, stroked and massaged his wounds. The pain eased for a moment, and he felt at peace once more. The jaundiced yellow face of the overseer forced him back to the cane piece. The overseer poked and prodded the blood stained boy shepherd to make sure he was not dead. It would have been a costly mistake. The planter would not have been amused at the death of his young expensive and newly acquired property. The plantation owner had instructed him, to buy as many healthy male and female slaves before the much talked about and hated Act for the abolition of slavery, was passed by Parliament and implemented.

The overseer barked orders to an elderly woman to clean up his wounds and return him to the cane piece without delay. He lay in the stuffy, windowless sick house and felt the raised skin where the cow whip had eaten into his flesh and made it raw. At dusk, his fellow Africans poked their heads into the sick house,

A slave being whipped in a cane piece. Adapted from an image published in La Moderna Epoke 4th World Issue Sept 14. aborginalwriter.wordpress.com

they asked their ancestors to make him better and guide him in the future.

Osei bathed his brow with the scented oils he had rung from the aromatic plants, which grew on the tiny house plot of his new family. The matron allowed him to stay in the hot house at night. He talked and chatted to Kufuo about the shepherding of their herd in Akin, and their stay on the solid basement floor in Elmina Fort. Kufuo did not respond. Osei was beside himself with worry and grief. How would he face the future without his dearest companion? Daily, the matron, cut the plump jagged fingers of the Aloe Vera plant, she placed its cold, sticky juice over his open flesh. Gradually, Osei began to notice a change in his friend; now and again his eyelids flickered when he mentioned their herd in Akin. Slowly, he was returning to them. The matron's daily practice brought the broken skin together and left Kufuo with the lifelong badge of slavery.

He did not stay too long in the sick house. The overseer sent him to the cattle pen to look after the animals, before returning to the cane piece when he was fully fit. The supervising of the animals very slowly eased his acute trauma. He became one with the animals giving them all his love. It was returned in abundance and with immense appreciation. The boy shepherd led them to the pasture to eat or fed them from the dried cane husks, the leftover molasses or scraps from their daily meal. Gradually, Kufuo tried to return to his old life on the scrublands of Akin with his herd of goats. At night, Kufuo and Osei would sit in front of the pen, they talked about the future. They spoke of the rumours that they would soon be freed when the Act of Abolition was passed in England.

They shared their hopes and wishes for the future, the same hopes and aspirations of all their brothers and sisters in the cane pieces, across 'The Enslaved World'. They would exit the plantations as soon as they could. Kufuo's induction into the brutality of plantation slavery occurred soon after he landed on the island's coast. The welts that covered Kufuo's tall, slender body, fuelled the fire of resistance to destroy slavery. Kufuo's desire for freedom consumed him each day in his work with the plantation animals. His experience of slavery and plantation life had cemented his resolve to smash the monstrous institution of slavery. The boy shepherd sought and worked towards the only alternative to slavery that he knew; freedom for himself and his people. To this end, Kufuo, Osei and the youth worked in unison. They worked at the plough, the crushing and extraction mills, the boiling and still houses. They also worked at the water wheel, the carts that carried the cane to and from the cane pieces, as well as in the animal pen.

The enslaved Africans had been preparing enthusiastically and practically for the ending of their enslavement. The talking drums had informed them of the events and persons who had been working to remove the chains and neck irons from their limbs. The island was their future; the hilly and mountainous, as well as the flat landscape, beckoned them. They knew what they had to do, they would create and invent their future. They kept their aspirations hidden in the recesses of their souls, waiting to fulfil and make them a reality.

However, their longing and craving for freedom and an independent future would be brutally snatched from them once more; as the anticipated Act of Abolition would once again intensify their enslavement. They cursed the treachery of the planters and their Parliament in England that had lengthened their enslavement while passing a law saying that they would be free. Instead of freeing them, they had extended their enslavement by an additional six long years. Six years of gruelling work and brutality called apprenticeships.

Their frustration and anger were vented in every corner of the compounds and plantations across the islands and the mainland. They dragged their heels, weeded and cut the cane at a snail's pace. Others laid down their hoes and cutlasses and refused to work. The overseers pulled out the ringleaders and placed them in chains and stocks in the middle of the cane piece. He strung some of them up on revolving racks; it broke their limbs and their spirit. The scorching sun drained away their life and resistance.

The resilient Africans were livid because they had wrenched their freedom from the planters. However, the planter's interests had once again stolen their right to liberty and total autonomy. They had been hardened by the treachery of slavery. They were a multi-dimensional people from across the African continent, so quickly they revised their expectations and plans for the future.

Slowly as night turned to day, their minds raced feverishly to identify routes out of their continued repression and into freedom. Immediately, they saw that the six-year apprenticeship opened a tiny yet possible window to find the alternative to slavery and, therefore, their unrestricted freedom. They would use the clause in the act, which allowed them to buy their way out of the apprenticeships, to finally put an end to their imprisonment.

As apprentices on the plantations, the Act of Abolition would force them to work for up to forty-five hours a week without pay, as before. They used the rest of their time productively and efficiently, to work on their small plots of land and provision grounds in the hilly and mountainous country. They wanted to squeeze their hours into four days, leaving them with three days to work for themselves. Production on the hilly ground as well as on their small plots grew fast and furiously. The apprentices cultivated food to supplement their miserly and decreased food rations; as well as more ground provisions to sell in the flourishing Sunday markets. They accumulated their savings to buy their freedom and future.

Swiftly, they put into practice the dimly remembered organisation of their motherland and their ancient communal practices. They would use these traditions and customs to confront the brazen injustices of slavery. Slavery had robbed generations of conscientious Africans, of their humanity, their liberty, their culture as well as their means of self-determination and advancement. The Africans began by renewing the tried and tested organisational practices of their ancestors that would prepare them for total freedom. Their savings would complement the over the hills and mountains railroad, out of the plantations to independent and sustainable futures. Once again, they turned to their senior Anancy for guidance and assistance.

"Brother Anancy," they said affectionately, "you have guided and sustained us throughout our ill-fated journey from our motherland. We have drawn on your courage and energy to maintain our morale during our captivity. We know and appreciate the fact that you hold in your person the wisdom, knowledge as well as the culture of our shared motherland. This has made you our guardian. You are our senior and our greatest resource.

Therefore, we will entrust to you our savings to look after and allocate without bias. Many of us had been putting aside money for the end of our enslavement, but now we will have to put aside even more money to buy our liberty, so our independence and future will be guaranteed. We also have on this estate and on all the plantations on the islands and the mainland; groups of men and women who will not wait another six years for their liberation. We do not know what obstructions the planters will put in place, to prolong our enslavement in six years' time. We want our freedom now, and we will move mountains to get it," they warned.

They all nodded in agreement.

"We know," they said, "that collective saving is the only way to meet head-on, the obstacles that the fiendish British Parliament have placed in our way. These impediments prevent us from becoming free and self-directing human beings in control of our future. Collective savings were the means by which our ancestors and community gained wealth and sustained their families and villages. We will revive these ancient saving clubs. We will show those born in the islands alternative ways of organising, that was lost to them through the monstrous regime of slavery."

"Anancy," they said, "each week we will bring a portion of our earnings from the goods we have harvested and sold from our plots, provision grounds or animal pen. Every week, there will be enough money to go towards buying one person's freedom when we get a big enough group to save. Our savings alone will not be sufficient. We will have to supplement our savings by borrowing from each other and drawing on the goodwill and generosity within our community," they told him.

Passionately, they continued.

"If we buy the freedom of twenty enslaved Africans on this plantation each year, it will be a great achievement. Anancy, you know how hard we have worked in our own time to get the money to start our Susu, partnership, our saving club. We are not averse to you helping us to make our money go a little further, by whatever means. We know Brother Anancy, we can depend on you, to enhance our liberation fund with your usual cunning and dexterity."

They all laughed knowingly.

CHAPTER 4

From slaves to apprentices

The agent perched his puffed up body in the rickety bamboo chair, his long and greying hair hung around his ballooning cheeks. His appearance reflected the squalidness of his surroundings. Fiercely, he clapped his hands and a young mulatto woman appeared and stood defiantly at his side. He ordered his breakfast, the young lady disappeared inside. Then, he poured rum into his chipped calabash and gulped it down as if it was water. The drunken soul strummed his fingers against the rough wooden chair as he waited for her return.

Presently, the young woman returned with a tin plate of coarse maize cakes, topped with pieces of seasoned and roasted boar's flesh. She shoved it under his nose and exited. The agent forced the food down his throat and ordered another bottle of rum. She chucked it under his jowl and vanished. His cheeks and nose glowed like a beacon on a dark winter's night, as untold quantities of rum slid down his gullet. He belched again and again, each time inflaming his bright red face, he clapped once more and the resentful young female gathered up the empty plates and left.

The gate creaked, the drunken agent looked towards it as his wobbling and blurry overseer approached him. Cautiously, the overseer shuffled towards him and looked uneasily at the mass sprawled in the crumbling chair. A whiff of rum hit him as he moved towards the shabby dwelling and agent. He knew he was in trouble. The mass stared at him, his eyes bore into his very soul as he belched and spurted the stale rum, from between his gritted teeth. His foul smelling mouth reeked as he leant forward; the overseer positioned himself not to inhale. Then, the dreaded rebuke he had been rehearsing answers for since he was summoned was flung at him, and it winded him.

"You almost killed one of those costly Negro boys," he snarled.

The agent spat out his fury at the cowering overseer and continued.

"This bloody Act will put an end to our God-given authority to buy and use these brainless Negroes, to work on our plantations. We have very few active Blackies left on this plantation; we have not been able to buy them at a favourable price since our ships stopped carrying them more than twenty years ago. Soon, we will not be able to buy any at all when the damn Act of Abolition is approved and put into practice. The Negro sluts don't have picannies anymore because the Obeah women kill them with their deadly potions. No matter how many of them we breed, they don't produce the goods. We want healthy Negro picannies to work in the cane pieces when they are older. We need them when we can no longer buy Negroes from the French and Dutch slave traders, under the cover of darkness," he admitted.

"Where on earth are we going to get more Negroes when the Act becomes law and is enforced? No, no, what has the Act called them, apprentices, yes but we all know that the Negroes will still be our slaves, regrettably for a trifling six years only. Our foolish Parliamentarians should have fastened them to us for another twenty years. That would have served us nicely. What will become of us and our plantations when they are freed at the end of the apprenticeships? I can assure you that they will be out of our plantations faster than cannon fire."

The agent sobered up for a minute and as if by doing so, the point he was about to make would have more weight.

"Those slave boys were the last ones I was able to buy before the supply dries up completely. It will be a couple of years before the slave traders return to our shores, and by that time the damn Act will be in place. Behold, you nearly killed one of them," he said gazing steadfastly at the grimy dirt floor of his shabby house.

"I was told to use whatever means necessary to secure as many male and female slaves that were available for this plantation, I have tried to carry out that instruction. Look at our position now, since the damn Act was thought up by those wigs and imbeciles and placed before Parliament. Daily, this half-breed repels my advances and shoves food in my face without fear. In the good old days, when our Negroes were just plain slaves she wouldn't dare. The talk of the Act of Abolition has made them even more fearless and forthright, in challenging our God-given authority as their masters," he grumbled.

"We have to be very thankful indeed that the Act of Abolition will secure our interests first and foremost. We can presume that the Negroes will remain in our cane pieces as apprentices for another six years only. If they had been freed straight away, it would have crippled us. It would have destroyed our plantations and the comfortable lifestyles of our betters. When the Negroes become aware of the full content of the Act, they will detest and loathe us deeply for their extended enslavement. They will be infuriated and resentful of the outcome, as it will crush their natural craving to be in control of their future and their lives. Heed my words now; our lives and our future will be in the greatest of danger when the content of the Act is widely known. It is, therefore, crucial that we maintain and enhance, our rigorous regime over them," the agent instructed.

"We know that they will fly from our cane pieces as soon as the apprenticeships are over or before if they have the means, as I have said before. If we are to survive, we must plan now the means by which they will be kept on the plantations after the apprenticeships have ended. I hate the bloody Negroes, they are never happy with their lot, they want their freedom now and this island for themselves. At this point in time, our survival and the requirements of our plantations come first, and that means keeping them alive to work for us after the apprenticeships end. We get very little work out of them now; they work mechanically in anticipation of the changes the Act will bring. They produce a fraction of the work since the rumours started. What will they produce after the law is changed? We know very well that the big plantations will indeed collapse if the Negroes are not kept on them, or close to them after the apprenticeships end.

We have mutilated and slain our slaves for our own entertainment, without any consequences to ourselves for nearly two centuries. That practice is now over; we cannot destroy our Negroes without destroying ourselves. We have to plan their future so that they continue to work for our benefit. That's what you should be doing right now, not beating the Negro boy to the point of death," he barked at the quaking overseer.

"Already, we have been told to seek out our most industrious and well-behaved slaves. We are to offer them fertile plots and favourable rents; so that they remain on our plantations at the end of the apprenticeships. We must look into it and prepare for the future, that must be our mission from now on," the agent told his trembling overseer. "Governor Sligo, has already shown us the way forward. He will free his slaves as soon as the Act is passed so he will have no apprentices. He is a cunning man indeed. Many of the planters and others, including myself, laughed at him and called him many names when we heard of his plans. We insulted his honour; we called him the father of the savages. However, he took no notice of us. But alas, now we see he was shrewdly thinking about tomorrow and his own future. We were the asses; we were thinking with our backsides while drinking rum," he wheezed.

"By freeing his slaves when the Act is passed, this very astute man has made sure he will always have labour for his plantation. His Blackies with help from those meddlesome Baptists will set up their own villages not far from his plantation. He will create an illusion of freedom, we must do the very same. I must say it again, Governor Sligo is indeed an intelligent man. He used his head instead of the whip and, therefore, he will keep the Negroes close by," the agent said looking threateningly at his overseer.

187

"But more importantly for us, this arrangement will keep down wages after the apprenticeships end, because of the abundant supply of Negro labour close at hand. This will benefit the governor; it will also be to our advantage. That's what you should be attending to right now, not whipping our slaves to near death. Planning the Negroes' exit from our plantation must be our priority, your chief concern from now on as it guarantees our future. Long may Governor Sligo live, he has given us the model for the future," he roared.

Cringing and bowing almost to the foul-smelling floor, the overseer apologised for his great error and assured the agent that it would not happen again.

"I will let it go this time,' he said, 'because I don't want to spoil our little arrangement. We need the Negroes even more now than our masters. Without them we will be planting and weeding our own little cane pieces very soon," he grinned uncomfortably.

The overseer bowed his lowest curtsey and backed out of the gate. Their secret arrangement over the years had given them money to buy two small animal pens nearby. They both had a couple of acres on which they grew sugarcane, which the enslaved Africans had been forced to take turns labouring in them in their few hours of rest and respite. He had plenty to think about. He would have to find ways to maintain their forced arrangement with the apprentices, so it remained viable and kept them in the lifestyle they had become used to.

The agent swaggered into the house; his young housekeeper was mending and darning his tattered breeches. He crept up behind her and placed his fat reeking body on top of her. Violently, she shoved him away; he staggered and almost fell on his knees. He stood upright, his legs gave way, and he tumbled forward and hit his head against a cask of rum. Slowly, tinges of crimson and blue spread across his face and body, it frightened her so she threw a bucket of water over him. It revived him for a moment. Then he vomited, swallowed some of it and fell onto the reeking floor. The agent lay very, very still and stiff. She ran from the shabby house screaming.

The overseer mooched back to the plantation. He had a lot of work to do to maintain their little arrangement. He had not thought about the effect, the Act would have on their forced agreement in the future. The words of the agent went around and around in his head. He thought about all those Negroes he had whipped and forced to dig, plant, weed and harvest his little cane piece close to Bax Hall plantation. The enslaved Africans had deeply resented spending hours of their rest days, on maintaining the small but demanding cane pieces. They had cursed and despised them because they had their own miniature and rocky plots to cultivate to feed themselves, their families and make a little money to trade in the Sunday markets.

In the future, it would be harder to get the Negroes to work on their modest, but demanding cane pieces and animal pens. He reflected on his way home. That night he lay in his little house, he thought and thought, it was a chilly night, and the clouds had deserted the night sky. A frosty wind blew across the plantation, the sleeping Africans shivered in their huts on top of the rocks, above the cane pieces. Next morning, they pulled up some familiar plants and boiled them until they had a thick and bitter green liquid. They drank it and went to the cane piece. The overseer sneezed and sneezed, in his little house it wobbled and shook violently.

CHAPTER 5

Resistance and an end to the apprenticeships

The rebellious Africans raged at the continued theft of their deliverance. They would buy their freedom and destroy the planters along with their plantations, and finally end their control over them.

Quickly and confidently, Kufuo, Osei and the younger generation embraced this crucial task. They were guided and supported by their elders and their senior Anancy. The boys' experience as enslaved Africans had been relatively brief in comparison to many of their elders. Every day, Kufuo and Osei dreamt of looking after their goat herd on the scrublands of Akin without restrictions. Day-by-day, their hatred of the apprenticeships grew. Their burning desire was to end their continued subjugation, as well as the re-enslavement of their brothers and sisters on the plantations on the islands and the mainland.

Each day, as they grazed and looked after the goats and other animals on the demanding hillsides, they talked and planned how to end the insufferable apprenticeships. In the evenings, by the compound fires they discussed with the elders the way forward. The elders smiled with pride as they saw the determination of the younger generation, to take on the struggle that they and their ancestors had so valiantly waged against the planters throughout their enslavement. They encouraged and urged the young men and women forward in their mission to end their continued repression. The youths were energised and stimulated into action.

Nightly, around the compound fires, the stories of the resistance in Africa of their ancestors were acted out to strengthen their resolve to end their extended enslavement. The stories of the Africans' resistance during the Atlantic crossing and on the plantations over the centuries were told and retold night after night. These stories strengthened their determination to end their enslavement.

They begged the elders to tell them the Anancy stories of their infancy and, in particular, the contribution of the great Sky God Nyame's son Anancy. He had throughout the centuries inspired and nurtured the grit and stamina of their ancestors, to rise up against slavery and end it. The folk tales of Africa and the Anancy stories served to organise and mask their subversion of plantation slavery from the planters and their accomplices. These were complemented by the stories of the African heroes and heroines of 'The Enslaved World', on the islands and the mainland. These stories told of the confrontation and courage of their ancestors against slavery in the cane pieces.

After the youth had prepared and watered their plots and provision grounds, they acted out the heroic stories of bravery and fearlessness around the compound fires, as their ancestors had done centuries before them. They performed the stories of resistance to slavery from the very beginning to honour those ancestors who had fought to end their enslavement. The courage and daring spirit of this generation would end the apprenticeships and slavery in all the British colonies and the world forever.

The young men competed with each other to act out the roles of, and keep alive the spirit of, the brave African warriors of the past; bold and daring Africans such as Juan de Bolas and his brave fighters. They had initially fought with the Spanish against the invasion of the island by the British in 1655. The British soldiers and adventurers had fled at the sight of these brave and fearless African warriors. The warriors had terrified them, so they turned and ran back to their boats. In a few leaps and bounds, Juan de Bolas' army overtook them. They towered above them with their sharp and glinting cutlasses and spears. The British soldiers trembled, quivered and begged for their lives. Juan de Bolas' men, seeing their quaking bodies and deathly white pallor, put them in boats and pushed them out to sea. Many of these British soldiers and adventurers returned to relatively flat islands like Barbados, without bands of African warriors lodged in the mountaintops.

The British government and their generals were determined to take control of the entire island to grow sugar, so meekly they sought out Juan de Bolas and begged his pardon for any unfortunate misunderstandings. Remorsefully, they stressed that they had no quarrel with the Africans in the mountains. However, they were furious with the Spanish King and his generals. They had broken an unwritten agreement, so they had to take the island by force. They impressed on him the fact that a King's verbal agreement was an unbreakable bond and, therefore, they would make the Spanish King keep his promise. They told him that the island was theirs, to roam freely if they helped them to make the Spanish King keep to their agreement.

Juan de Bolas agreed after considering the situation. He gathered his warriors and together they attacked the remaining Spanish fortress against the British in the mountains. Arnaldo de Ysassi, the last Spanish governor and general on the island resisting the British invasion, fled to Cuba in a boat after a brutal five-year war. When most of the Spanish resistance had been driven from the island or were killed; the British general plotted how to enslave Juan de Bolas and his African warriors. They called a meeting between themselves and Juan de Bolas and offered them wine and many delicacies from Britain. As the free Africans ate, danced and laughed with their hosts, the British army surrounded them. Juan Bolas had anticipated the trickery of the British. He had also left some of his men close to the camp. Juan de Bolas and his men fought their way out of the British enclosure and killed many soldiers, the rest fled. Juan de Bolas and his men returned to the mountains and fought the British invaders as they spread out over the flat coastal lands and set up sugar plantations. Later, the British general and governor made a deal with Juan de Bolas, to stop attacks on their plantations and control hostile sections of the mountain community.

Juan de Bolas and his men became the heroes of the youth because they had been expert cattle ranchers, hunting the wild boars across the island. They had also looked after vast herds of goats and other animals on the ranches of the Spanish invaders. Importantly, they had established mountaintop settlements for the future. In their mock battles, Kufuo and Osei took on the roles of their brave ancestors and honoured them for their courage and determination in creating an alternative to plantation slavery in the mountains.

If the Africans had produced great male leaders, they also had their great female heroines and warriors. The apprentices celebrated the African women who gave them life and reared them in the most horrendous conditions. These women grew the crops to nourish and sustain them and they worked in the cane pieces too, they were also brave fighters and tacticians. The women and young girls vied with each other to play the various roles of Nanny of the Maroons, their fearless warrior queen. A young girl named Esi had distinguished herself, playing the role of Nanny and her daring warriors. Carefully, she had listened to the stories told about Nanny around the compound fires. She had practiced and practiced the actions, mannerisms and traits of this great female warrior when playing with the other children. Respectfully, she had approached the elders and asked if she could play the role of warrior Nanny, as usually the female parts were played by young boys. At a performance one of Nanny's fiercest battles against the British army, she excelled in the role. Convincingly, she used the daring strategies of Nanny to guide her troops into battle and to victory against the British army. After such a memorable performance, Esi was referred to as the little Nanny of the Maroons in the compounds.

Kufuo and Osei admired the strength and courage of little Nanny. They always ensured that she was included in the staging of the great achievements of their ancestors. During the Christmas celebrations, they travelled the island with the Junkanoo bands performing the feats of their brave and gallant ancestors. Next, they questioned the elders about the other brave leaders who had fought to end their enslavement. Proudly, the elders told them the story of Tacky, who had led a major revolt against slavery in 1760. The youth challenged each other to act out Tacky's uprising. They also staged the Christmas rebellion in which they stressed the role of the enslaved Africans in hiding and feeding their emancipator when the British army hunted high and low for him. The young men and women were eager to demonstrate, that when all the enslaved Africans on the plantations across the island worked together, they had forced the planters and their government to pass the Act of Abolition.

Juan de Bolas, Nanny, Tacky, Deacon Sam Sharp, Cuffy, Bussa, Quamina and thousands of unnamed Africans had died resisting slavery, thus creating a future for Kufuo, Osei, Esi and the youth. Without delay, the young people set about overturning the apprenticeships, to bring about their total liberation. The defiant Africans, their elders and their senior Anancy, would be at the forefront of the battle to end the apprenticeship system and bury plantation slavery forever.

CHAPTER 6

Anancy goes gambling

Christmas was just around the corner. The Backra, who chose to spend time on the island, opted for this season because it was cool, windy and hospitable. The threat of hurricanes had finished at the end of November. Some of the cane had been cut, but the remainder had to be harvested and the cane pieces prepared for the next growing season.

The first batch of rum was in the process of being distilled, bottled and bulked shipped back to England, in the favourable sailing winds. Smaller amounts were sold to the white settlers in North America and Canada. These encouraging conditions allowed the planters to cast a wary eye over their plantations while attending to any outstanding details with their agents and overseers.

Away from their families and acquaintances, the planters took the opportunity to liven up their idle, tedious and corrupt lives. At the same time, they plotted how they could steal more than forty-five hours a week of unpaid labour from their apprentices. They indulged in bouts of excessive drinking as well as gambling. These were some of the ways in which they lived their miserable lives. Fortunes and plantations were lost and mortgaged to the Portuguese-Jewish money-lenders on the island at the end of these sessions. The house Africans prepared the food, drink and entertainment for these miserable creatures. They existed because they had inherited one or more plantations from their parents or a distant relative, very few of them had set up sugar estates using their own resources.

The house Africans knew every detail of the planters' lifestyles. They knew their whims and immorality. Diligently, they attended to these, at this time of the year because they provided excellent possibilities for food for their Christmas celebrations. In the compounds, the festive menus were already written. The Backra planned the next gambling sessions and the invitations were sent out with the house Africans. The first session would begin on Christmas Eve after the Backra had been to church to thank their God for their apprentices, plantations and the fortunes that he had so kindly bestowed on them.

I, Anancy man and spider, thought long and hard about our new situation. Before 1834, my extended family had run away from the plantations to the mountaintops of the islands. On the mainland, they had fled to the swampy forests and mountains where the Backra were afraid to go. Now, the solution to our liberation must be informed by our changing circumstances. My brothers and sisters on the plantations, like the Maroons in the mountains, knew they could not wait for the Backra to free them. They would exit the plantations as soon as they could. The apprentices used their small plots and the money from them, as their ticket to freedom and autonomy. I heard of the planned poker game; I also knew of the drunkenness and vice that was a feature of the Backras' celebrations. These situations had always presented opportunities for us in the past. Now they could aid our desire for freedom too. I took my opportunity; I would be at the heart of the Backras' poker game and carousing. My brothers and sisters had made me their bank manager, as well as their money-spinner; I would boost their savings.

Hibiscus flowers along with their ruby red seedpods were used to decorate the banqueting table. The resourceful Africans used these ruby red petals to make the most delicious Christmas wine, boiled with ginger and laced with nutmeg, cinnamon and rum. The house Africans placed a roasted boar, a roasted goat, half a shank of boiled beef, roasted and stuffed birds, chickens with chestnut and other sweetmeats imported from England for four gluttons. A cask of rum stood in a corner of the room to replenish empty jugs and goblets along with a selection of wines and other spirits. The delicious and sober fruits of the island were placed at the back of the room because they did not have the strength to induce drunkenness and vice.

Four Backra had accepted the invitation to spend the festive season together, away from the insufferable cold weather in England. The cold snow-frosted days that seeped into their stiff and ageing bones causing them unbearable aches and pain. Backra one was a tall, spindly man of about fifty years, with a grey receding hairline. He was an Oxbridge graduate with a flourishing and successful business in England. He had inherited his six hundred and fifty-acre plantation, in the north east of the island, from an uncle. This was his second visit to the isle. He quite liked the island, and his plantation, because they were so unlike the stiff and constraining morality of the society he had been born into.

Backra two was a white Jamaican by birth, only forty years of age with a protruding belly and a strawberry face. He looked much older than his years. His great-grandfather was one of the first planters on the island after the British invaded and took it from the Spanish in 1655. He had one of the biggest plantations on the island. He had no desire to live in a land that was so cold it froze your body parts. This planter had an enjoyable life in Jamaica, his wife resided in Spanish Town, the capital of the island while he lived on his plantation doing whatever he liked. He was one of the luckiest of men because, while most Backra wilted under the heat and were prone to tropical diseases such as yellow fever and malaria, he suffered no such afflictions. He counted the days to the next festivities with his peers.

Backra three was the youngest of all, only thirty years of age with a very pleasant manner. He was full of good intentions to improve his plantation, with some of the newer methods of cultivating cane. This was his first time in Jamaica. He had inherited his estate from a distant cousin. New to the island, the established Backra saw it as their duty to break him into the ways of the Backra. They had to forge a solid front against the rebellious Africans. This was vital because the bold Africans in St Domingue had fought for centuries, first against the Spanish and then the French.

Their rebellion of 1791 had sent shock waves through the Backra community in Jamaica. St Domingue was only a hundred or so miles from Jamaica at their nearest point. The planters had had to rescue hundreds of their fellow cane piece owners from there, after the fearless Africans, led by their Generals Toussaint L'Ouverture and Jean Jacques Dessalines, took their island for themselves. In 1804, they declared their island an independent country. These events in St Domingue ensured that the Backra kept a tighter rein on the Africans on their plantations.

They were hosted by the oldest of the four; he was also a Jamaican by birth. He was short and stocky with a pockmarked and wrinkled face; his brother had been killed in the slave uprising of 1831-32, led by Deacon Sam Sharpe. He had not managed to find the African, who had murdered his brother, so the rebellious Africans on his plantations paid for this daring act. Twenty were hung as an example to the others of their fate if they ever challenged his authority.

Daily, the host, had terrorised them to instil fear and break their resistance to slavery. He intimidated the labouring Africans with his whip and his two bloodhounds. At regular intervals, he would set out at different times on his slave patrol. On these rounds he took with him two huge bloodhounds, they were trained to devour anything and anyone he asked them to. No matter how hard the enslaved Africans tried to avoid his lethal circuits, the Backra always found a lonely soul out on some errand.

The host had made sure that an African would be out on a task, then he stalked them with his bloodhounds, and when his victim was at their most terrified, he let them loose. They were pinned to the floor by the enormous dogs, while he stood over the petrified souls quizzing them as to why they should be spared. This paranoid individual ordered them to tell him of any plots, or rebellions that were being planned on his plantation. Most of the terrified Africans passed out from fright before they could answer, then he called off the dogs and continued his walk.

At the gathering, he told his assembled guests that their Negroes should never be trusted because, if they had the opportunity, they would murder them in their beds. He reminded them that the Negro slaves in Haiti had driven out the planters and had made their country independent. Their president had, he thought, financed the rebels in South America, led by Simon Bolivar. This allowed them to drive the Spanish planters and government from some of their colonies.

Their host told them that he had no doubt in his mind that the Negro president in Haiti, and the Baptists from abroad, had financed and encouraged the Western Rebellion, which had killed his beloved brother. Haiti's president he believed had encouraged their slaves to drive them into the sea and free themselves. He congratulated himself, his fellow planters and the British government for putting a stop to the devilish plans of the Negro President in Haiti, to free their slaves on this island and the mainland. The prompt and decisive action by the British government and the army had saved the islands and the mainland for them.

Eagerly, their host reminded them of his activities with his dogs and encouraged them to follow suit. It was their duty to make sure that their slaves, now apprentices would know that they would always be in charge, even though, the Act specified that they would be freed in six years' time. He had a gratifying life on his plantation, his English wife gave him respectability. However, when he was alone on his plantation he had the time of his life. He tried to hide the fact that he was obsessed with the beauty of African and Mulatto women. The host was surrounded by women of great beauty, and he tortured and raped them constantly. No African woman on his plantation was free from his gruesome desires, he used his dogs to terrorise them. The plantation owner enjoyed the festive season most of all when the company of other Backra gave added pleasures such as gambling. It also offered the opportunity to increase his fortune, as well as his plantation.

Plates and goblets were placed on a table next to the card table, the house Africans left the room. The host tore a leg from the wild hog and took a bite, then he placed the remainder on the table. He invited his guests to do the same, he clapped, and an African returned and filled their goblets and disappeared. They continued to eat and drink from the banqueting table. The first few games were friendly as they laid guineas upon guineas and called each other's bluff. As the rum numbed their senses, noisily they slapped guinea coins onto the table and increased their bets. Now and then, they barked at the house Africans to bring more rum and dancing girls.

Anancy entered the gambling den; during each game, he slid guinea coins off the table and carefully placed them in his pouch. Each time a game ended, the Backra quarrelled bitterly about the amounts on the table, each swearing that they had put the required amounts down. The host chided his guests and reminded them that they were all having a splendid time. However, it seemed to him that the overflowing liquor was numbing their senses.

"I think," he said, "the rum has impaired our fingers and the guineas are finding it difficult to come out of our purses. What are a few guineas among friends? Let's play until all our pockets are empty. Our apprentices, no, no our slaves because that's what they really are, will soon fill them with more guineas tomorrow," he wheezed and snorted into his rum.

"Let's play another round," begged the host, "this time without the demon rum. These delicious fruits from my grounds will help to keep us awake, to see clearly into our purses."

More awake than ever, the house Africans were called to observe the amounts placed on the table by each player. Sober as judges, the Africans kept a log of the guineas placed on the table. They played their last cards. The victor claimed his guineas, only to find that some were missing again. The host grabbed hold of the Africans and one by one he turned them upside down; no guineas fell from their pockets to his annoyance. He ordered more wine and rum and tried to explain away their problem.

He told his guests that although the planters had frequently slaughtered those Negroes, who they believed to be Obeah men and women on their plantations, new ones appeared and replaced them immediately. He concluded that they had stolen and were taking guineas from the card table. However, in the cold light of day the planters blamed their losses on their blurred senses, brought about by drinking too much rum during the game. They would play another game before returning to England, to settle debts and visit their newly won plantations.

I, Anancy, returned to the compound with a broad grin, as well as a sizable haul of guineas for the freedom fund. Every guinea taken from the card table, compensated for zero of the cost of the labour of the exploited and petrified Africans on the plantations over the centuries. There would be more occasions to gain from such a profitable stunt in the future. The freedom fund would stand alongside the exodus to the mountaintops.

CHAPTER 7

Kufuo saves the animals and the island

Kufuo did not return to the cane piece after his beating by the wizened overseer. Fortunately, for the enslaved Africans he caught the fever at the start of the dry season. He tossed and turned in his little house as fever impaired his brain and his senses. In his delirious state, he saw the ghosts of the Africans that he had whipped to death, dancing by a newly dug grave. They danced and beckoned him to enter the hole that they had so carefully prepared for him.

In those moments he screamed.

"I am a God fearing man. My God will guide me through this little fever. The Negro doctor is on his way from the Bay with a bag full of bitter wood from the Quassia tree. He will make me better," he coughed.

Fever consumed him, so the African matron sponged him down. The drought in the region delayed the Negro doctor for more than a week. Slowly, his wizened face and body shrank until his skull and bones could be seen through his transparent skin. He lay on his soaking coir bed in the scorching heat, where the breeze refused to enter. He screamed as the fever ate into his body and slowly life left his earthly remains.

Kufuo's induction into the animal pen with its array of animals very slowly eased his acute distress. He bonded with the animals, and although there were few goats in the pen, it did not matter. He stroked the coat and faces of the horses and cows. They loved his caring touch. Soon, it was noticeable to everyone on the plantation that the animals were well cared for and, therefore, produced more work. Kufuo's achievements with the animals were short lived, as a severe drought in the West and Northwestern parts of the island affected the plantations severely. The water from the great river that powered the water wheel was almost dry. Water trickled along the pipes leading into the estate and dried up before it reached the water wheel. The mediocre management by the agent and overseer meant that there were no plans in place to find other sources of water.

In Akin, Kufuo could handle such a situation with ease. He would draw on the collective knowledge and teaching of his people, to ensure that shepherds knew how to deal with and prevent damage to the cattle in times of water shortage and extreme drought. Here he had to learn about this new terrain. He needed to know where substantial reserves of water could be found underground. Kufuo rose to the challenge drawing on his knowledge from Akin. He questioned the wheelwrights about equipment to search for inaccessible water underground. They found a few tools and began digging up the earth. Day in, day out, the hole got wider and deeper without success.

A week passed, and the new overseer and agent ordered that the animals in the pen had to be slaughtered to conserve the remaining water for the animals working in the cane pieces and mill house. Kufuo was devastated. This made him work harder, he begged for more time, the agent refused. He continued working in the few hours of rest he had away from the pen. Sometimes, it was almost impossible to see Kufuo, Osei and the other youths' bodies almost buried underground. They worked every evening and well into the night until late one night Kufuo felt the hardened ground giving way to soft, moist earth. He was frightened that he would sink into the water beneath his feet.

Quickly, he ordered those above to pull up the rope that had suspended him below the ground. Next morning, he instructed his fellow workers to tie the heaviest logs together to use as a battering ram, to dislodge the remaining soil. The logs sunk through the wet ground and floated on the water. They were hurriedly withdrawn, and a leather bucket replaced them. It fell hundreds of metres underground and hit the water and floated on top of it. The bucket was hauled to the surface and stones carefully placed inside it. Effortlessly, it glided to the bottom and hit the water with a noisy splash. The pen gang dragged the clean sparkling water to the surface and with cupped hands drank buckets. Work on the plantation stopped, as all the excited Africans proceeded to the hole in the ground to see the miracle water.

A celebration followed as the women danced and shrieked in the traditional African way. They thanked the ancestors for giving them this exceptional son, who had found water deep beneath the earth so quickly. They did not return to the cane piece until late the next day. The agent and overseer were delighted but concerned. They discussed what to do about the situation, should they inform the Backra abroad or take the credit for Kufuo's work. Rapidly, the news spread across the drought-stricken area. Many delegations from agents and overseers arrived to inspect the miracle water and see how they could benefit. Kufuo's genius had gone beyond the plantation. It was so widely talked about by the adoring Africans that the overseer, agent and planter could not take the credit for it and steal Kufuo's glory.

The Backra for the plantation sent a message to his agent and overseer. He instructed them to allow the stonemasons to work with Kufuo and the youths to find suitable sites to dig up and build wells until the rains came. These deep wells would be the alternate source of water on the plantations at all times. The remaining animals were saved as well as his sisters and brothers. Kufuo received his freedom and 100 guineas as a reward for his resourcefulness.

Soon after some engineers arrived from England. They discussed the kinds of machinery that could be built in the factories of Birmingham, Manchester and Sheffield, to speed up the building of wells in the islands and the mainland colonies. It was never acknowledged in the textbooks of the industrial revolution, that many inventions were first pioneered by many talented Africans on the plantations during slavery. The books said that British engineers had developed and made them to improve the lives of the Negro slaves, working in the cane pieces.

The jubilant Africans were filled with pride and generosity. Naturally, they added Kufuo's achievements to their oral tradition. They sang to babies and children around the compound fires about Kufuo an ordinary shepherd boy, who had saved all the animals and the people on the plantations, as well as the island.

CHAPTER 8

Kufuo's freedom restored

That night, Kufuo lay in his little stone house and wondered at his good luck and the advantages he had created for himself. The Backra could not deny Kufuo's innovation and contribution to his plantation, so he rewarded him in the only way he knew how. He gave him a miserly 100 guineas which he knew would come back to him very soon. Next morning, Kufuo was keen to do the necessary business, so he could leave the plantation and never return. He gave the 100 guineas to the agent to secure the freedom of Esi, the young woman he had asked to marry him. Together, they walked from Bax Hall plantation to begin a new life, as free Africans and human beings.

As they left the estate, they talked about their future and the options available to them. Esi told him she had often seen him from the boiling house opening, when he was taking the animals out to graze, at the crack of dawn. She had wanted to talk to him about their storytelling sessions, around the compound gatherings long, long ago. She had also wanted to stroke the coats of the animals. Kufuo told her that he had noticed a head at the boiling house's window a few times, but he did not know that it was hers. He shared with her the fact that he had always thought her performances as warrior Nanny had been brilliant, so he could never forget her.

Kufuo also told her that he did not want to leave the animals behind because he was worried that they would not be satisfactorily looked after. The caring for the animals would be given to the young boys on the plantation. They were so young that they could not be expected to look after the animals properly, without proper supervision. They should be at school or playing with children of their own age, so he had asked the Backra if Osei could manage the cattle pen. He knew the diligence of his herding partner from Akin. He was very surprised and pleased when his request was granted. Esi and Kufuo left the plantation to secure their future.

They proceeded to the Moravian mission some miles away, where they could get some paid work and shelter. The missionaries had challenged the institution of slavery from the time they landed on the island, in the middle of the 18th Century, in some form or other. They, and much later, the Baptist and Methodist missionaries, had supported the movement to end the slave trade on the islands and the mainland. They became the enemies of the established Church of England, the government and most of all the planters. They supported the free Africans by buying small pieces of land where they could work the land collectively; this practice grew rapidly after 1838. These missionaries intended to win the hearts and soul of all the enslaved African population for their God one day.

At the end of the harvest, the free Africans sold their produce and divided their earnings among themselves. They paid some monies to the churches so that they could buy more land for free Africans to work. Free Africans likewise pooled their funds and bought small parcels of land in the hilly and rocky areas of the island, to grow food to feed themselves and their families. These Africans sold their surplus produce in the Sunday markets, along with the Africans still working on the plantations. The rewards were small, but it was a start and with prudent savings they could one day, buy more flat, as well as fertile land, either to grow food or keep animals.

On the smaller islands without a hilly and mountainous landscape, the Africans just left the plantations and made their houses wherever they found strips and scraps of empty land. This greatly alarmed the planters, who were intent on keeping them close to the cane pieces as a cheap and readily available workforce after the apprenticeships ended.

Kufuo and Esi discussed how they would save for the future. They agreed that they could not do it alone, as it would take too long so they would join an African saving club, a Susu or Pardner. She told Kufuo that if they could get enough land they could keep goats, then they would be able to supply their fellow Africans when they had celebrations or special events. She would help to look after them.

Next day after work, the pair set off for a small free village, some miles from the mission. They were met by an elder, who offered them refreshments and a comfortable place under a gigantic Silk Cotton tree.

"I can guess why you are both here," a headman laughed loudly.

"You have come to give your hard earned money to our senior Anancy. I can't understand why everyone wants to give him their hard earned guineas," he laughed.

"So there are many people interested in our saving club?" asked Kufuo eagerly.

"Yes, yes, we have enrolled over 40 Africans in our saving club, the numbers grow daily. Our elder Anancy will need an enormous pot to keep all the guineas we are so keen to give him, as well as those he took from the planters. The money seems to grow and grow," he chuckled.

I, Anancy, joined them under the tree and told them of my delight at the response to the saving club. I told them that there were 20 passionate brothers and sisters saving to buy their freedom. Another 20 free Africans were saving to buy land. It pleased me greatly to see so many Africans working together to free themselves. Our efforts would hasten the end of plantation slavery because no free person would re-enter the plantations in their present form.

"The planters," I told them, "have kept us on the plantations as apprentices to continue to benefit from our unpaid work. At present, they cannot get any more enormous quantities of unpaid workers to run their cane pieces profitably. We replaced the Taino people, as well as the white indentured servants who could not work at the speed the planters hankered after to sustain their income and profit. The slave masters have worked our brothers and sisters to death to keep their plantations and wealth."

"They have in the distant past been able to replace them from the never-ending pool of our brother and sisters, being stolen and shipped daily from the continent. Now, we are challenging their future survival, as more and more of us become free and leave the plantations. The Backra will make it hard for us to get fertile and productive land away from the plantations. They will not allow us to compete with them as small farmers, as this will threaten the continued existence of their plantations. I can assure you all that they are busy making plans for us right now, to secure their interests when we are finally freed," he observed.

"They will find ways of making sure we remain on their plantations after the apprenticeships have ended. They have plans to prevent us from owning flat and fertile land as well as moving away from the plantations. We know how their minds work, and we will overcome them now by working together. Our plan is the following: each week we collect money from the members of our saving club. We will give the money to one person or persons who will use it to purchase their freedom, or buy land. In a year, there will be a significant number of Africans on the plantations buying their freedom, while those who are already free will buy land to farm. When the news of our successful saving club is widely known, it will attract more of our brothers and sisters and together we will empty the plantations before 1840," he assured them.

"There are one or two free villages set up by freed Mulattos and our free community. There is another free community in Sligoville, it was the first free village on the island. This free village was set up by Governor Sligo at the passing of the Act of Abolition. He has no apprentices. The Africans are now free and they have the possibility to buy land and work collectively or individually. As I have said before the planters and their government, have always arranged everything to suit their interests rather than our own.

Governor Sligo and the government he represented, knew that we would not stay on the plantations and pay enormous rents for the meagre and rocky plots; they begrudgingly allowed us to live on and grow food. By freeing his slaves and allowing a free village to be set up close to his plantation, he has kept the Africans close by. He has ensured a cheap and constant supply of labour," he told them.

He continued.

"On the island of Antigua, the planters freed their slaves when the Act was implemented in 1834. However, the majority of our brothers and sisters had to remain on the plantations because the Backra owned all the land. There were no rocky pieces of land that they didn't want, so the Africans had to remain on their plantations and work for miserable wages. Other planters have told their agents to give favourable conditions to those Africans they regard as good, obedient workers so they will remain on their plantations. They intend to divide us yet again, as they divided us and the Maroons. We must never forget how the planters and their allies used our brothers and sisters in the mountaintops to return us to the plantations, therefore restricting our attempts to liberate ourselves. They were also used to hunt our brothers and sisters who tried to end slavery. It was a Maroon tracker who hunted Tacky our brave leader and shot him, he would have ended slavery over seventy years ago," he told them gravely.

"We must learn these lessons, we must never allow them to be repeated. I know that we, as a dignified and proud people, do not want to work on their plantations or in their free villages. We do not intend to be exploited as cheap labour when we liberate ourselves. We want to be independent and self-governing. We want to be in control of our lives and future after more than three centuries. Our saving clubs will give us the means to empty the plantations. We will retake control of our lives and destiny," he informed them.

"When the planters do not have our free labour in large quantities, the plantations will collapse. They will have to sell the land to us whether they want to or not. The competition from sugar beet, as well as our never-ending uprisings, have helped to push down the price of sugar, making some plantations unprofitable. In the future mark my words, the planters will be forced to cut up their land and sell it to us to pay their debts. There is enough land in the hilly areas around the plantations, to provide smallholdings for our people at present. However, in six years' time, if all the apprentices are freed we will have a problem finding land for everyone," he warned.

"We must plan for our total liberation now, by buying our freedom whatever the cost. This will prevent any tricks the planters have to extend our enslavement, as they did with the Act of Abolition. At the moment, we can only buy the land they don't want. However, as more and more of us buy our way out of the plantations, they will collapse when our free labour is no longer available. Then we will be able to purchase the land that rightly belongs to the Taino people and ourselves. We will not wait another six years," he declared defiantly.

"The planters have been paid four times over. Our ancestors were forced to work as free labour since the beginning of the Sixteenth Century. At present, the apprentices work up to forty-five hours a week for free. The Backra have been promised hundreds of guineas to release us in six years' time. Now, we pay them to free ourselves, with the money we earn from working in our own time. Our hard earned money is guarded in the day by a talking bird and by night by a roaring lion," he giggled.

Enthusiastically, the audience cheered their senior for his wise and insightful words. Kufuo and Esi took their leave and promised to return the following week with their money. They were looking around for a suitable piece of land to buy, lease or rent. He also wanted to marry and celebrate heartily with his sisters and brothers. Esi told him that she would only marry him when they owned a plot of land; then they could begin to earn a living and build a little house. She agreed with him that they should return to the mission and work together to secure their future.

CHAPTER 9

Esi

Everyone was attracted to Esi's smooth and shiny Ebony skin, her huge dark brown eyes and short-cropped hair. She was short with a slight bodily frame, yet she was strong. She worked in the boiling house supervising the making of the sugar. The boiling house was a furnace, so she was greatly admired for her ability to work in such hard and harsh conditions. Esi managed the sugar making processes, from the time the cane juice was boiled and skimmed several times to remove the molasses. This left gleaming white sugar crystals, which were dried and bagged before being stored and shipped.

Esi was born on the plantation and was known as a Creole, the term used to describe those born on the plantations in 'The Enslaved World'. Her parents were house Africans; they had wanted her to work in the big house too. However, she had refused. She was strong willed and hated the close confines of the plantation house; where the Africans were at the mercy of the planters and their families for more than twenty-four hours a day. She worked for some years in the big house fetching and carrying for her parents. Then, she decided she wanted another job away from the big house, but not in the cane piece.

When a male worker in the boiling house was severely injured, while processing the cane juice into sugar, Esi volunteered to take his place in the dangerous furnace. Her parents begged her not to go, but she went anyway. She worked in the boiling house until Kufuo bought her freedom and asked her parents if they could marry when it was possible. Her parents did not object to

Kufuo because they saw in him a steady worker with good prospects for the future. They knew of the work he had done transforming the lives of the work animals, his reputation had gone before him. They were proud to have a daughter married to such a man. They would be looked up to within their community.

Esi loved Kufuo because he was a hard and honest worker. She also felt he was fair-minded because most of the time he did not force his opinions on her. Kufuo was willing to ask her what she thought, and she liked this. They would make a great partnership when they were married. They had known each other since she was a young girl. She had enjoyed following Osei, Kufuo and the other youngsters around the plantations as they performed the heroic tales of their heroes and heroines, who had fought to end their enslavement. Now, they worked together at the mission and pooled their small wages, allowing them to plan how they would save for a plot of land and their wedding.

After their marriage, they had paid down on a small sloping plot and this determined their roles. Kufuo set out for the hilly and mountainous peaks capped by the drifting mist, with his few animals to find good grazing spots. Esi was left with the care of the house and the plot. Daily, she rose to the challenge, she cleaned out the two rooms and hoarded the droppings from the animal's room and surveyed her sloping plot to see how she could get the best from it. The emerging farmer worked below the pen scratching away at the sloping ridges, to find indentations to build up to grow food.

Gradually, she identified areas where she could build up with flat stones, wood and soil to make beds to grow food. It was a complicated job, but Esi knew what she had to do. They were free, and the rewards of their hard work would be theirs, not the Backras'. The hillside farmer collected mountains of soil and ash from the fires, as well as dung from the animals all around. Soon, the farmer had enough material to make deep enough terraces, she planted seedlings on their slanting land. Water was not a problem, as the wild forests around and above the plot attracted the rain during some part of the day. Most of the rain trickled down onto her plot threatening to wash away her precious soil.

The promising young farmer made seed beds next to the house and plaited bamboo reeds around them, then placed the seeds in them from the mission. When they germinated, Esi put them in the terraces and planted beans and peas that would grow quickly to provide proteins to supplement their meals. She planted Callaloo, a fast-growing vegetable that was part of the Africans' staple diet. The crop benefited from the rainwater that persistently fell onto the terraces. It grew profusely, and Esi was able to repay her friends with fresh bundles of this very delicate green vegetable, each week for their Sunday breakfast. When the beans, peas and scallion were trailing, she improvised ways of securing them to the slope using bamboo branches, as well as poles.

Next, the evolving farmer turned her attention to growing ground provisions, yams, sweet potatoes and dasheen all needing rich and deep soil in which to grow. She built mounds of soil hedged in by rocks, then nestled the fledgeling plants and yam heads inside. Every day, she received visitors who admired her good work. Some brought cho-cho and other vegetables like Pak Choi. These plants were introduced into the islands by the Indian and Chinese indentured labourers, brought from India and China respectively to work on the floundering sugar plantations. They grew readily from the abundance of water seeping down onto the slope.

Soon, Esi was recognised on the hillside as an experienced and prosperous farmer. Generously, she accepted all the compliments. She knew she had to find ways of growing more crops, to trade in the well-established Sunday markets. She also needed money to keep up their payments to the saving club, the Pardner so more Africans could buy their freedom.

Esi knew the task ahead, so she sought out every opportunity to learn new ways of improving her miniature farm. She had a small circle of women friends. These were mainly the ancient matrons who had lived in both Africa and the islands. They always had something to show or tell her to improve her sloping farm. They brought herbs and strong smelling plants and advised her where and how to grow, dry and store them to use in times of sickness and disease.

When the women finished helping Esi with her work on the hillside, they would sit in the shade of the little stone house. Akua, the old matron, would tell them about her life in Africa. She told them about the culture and traditions of their distant motherland and how the land was owned collectively by the people in each village and region. The matron talked about the rites of passage for the young and the role of the elders in helping to achieve them. She spoke of the powerful forces of the natural world and the many ceremonies that were dutifully performed, to pacify and demonstrate their respect for them. Akua told them about the many people and things she had seen on the plantations.

She always ended with the Anancy stories. She told them how Anancy the son of the Great African Sky God, had worn down their enemies the slave masters. He had been at the centre of the slaves' and apprentices' resistance to their enslavement and the pursuit of their freedom. Often, she told them the Anancy stories of her childhood, under the huge branches of spreading Silk Cotton trees in the compounds at night. Akua was passing on the wisdom and culture of her motherland to another generation.

CHAPTER 10

The wedding

Kufuo had secured his freedom from the plantation through his own efforts and intelligence. He had also obtained the freedom of his wife to be Esi. He had wanted to do more for his brothers and sisters who worked with him in the animal pen, but it wasn't possible. He would encourage them to join Anancy's saving club, the Pardner. They had both paid money into the saving club and Anancy had told them that they could have twenty guineas in six months' time. They were delighted, and Esi had encouraged him to buy some land to start an animal pen of his own. She had argued that once the animal pen was up and running they could save for their wedding.

Kufuo had argued that slavery had robbed them of, and suppressed nearly all of the traditions and practices of their motherland. This had left them with behaviours that were at odds with their African heritage and traditions. He would try to restore as many of their African traditions as he could. He argued that now that he was a free person, he would not continue in the ways the Backra had forced on them during their enslavement. They would be married in the traditional African way as far as this was possible. They would use any leftover money to seek out a plot they could afford, for an animal enclosure. A date was set for the wedding, and the preparations began. Their wedding would mark the revival of their African traditions and heritage in 'The Enslaved World'. The African family and ancestors would be there to bless and celebrate this marriage.

Hundreds of invitations were sent out to the elders of the communities using their communication systems. Saturday and

Sunday would be best as the Backra would be counting their money on Saturday and be in church on Sunday. Cotts Hall Maroon settlement was hired for the wedding. They would all be free to attend away from the prying eyes of the overseers and planters. The guest lists grew longer and longer. Soon four hundred guests were invited, it would take all their savings, but it was worth it. In their motherland, no expense was spared on such occasions. They also knew that their guests would find ways of giving something towards the wedding celebrations. Often they brought, livestock, fruits and ground provision as well as equipment to furnish the banqueting table. They would have to plan carefully, to include these valued gifts into the wedding preparations and celebrations.

Esi retired with the women to sort out her bridal wear and decorations. They agreed that they were free to recreate their version of traditional African bridal wear. They dyed white cloth into the vibrant colours of the island's soil. This cloth would be Esi's bridal wear. The women cut strips of cloth to wrap her head and flowers to adorn the head cover. They prepared clothes for the children and adults who would accompany the bridal parade. Then, the women made their outfits so that they would not upstage the bride. They decorated two broom handles to use at the end of the ceremony.

Kufuo and Osei set off for Cotts Hall to order the food and venue for the wedding ceremony. Cotts Hall would be relatively easy to get to for their visitors coming from across the island. The captain and chief took their order for the marriage feast. They ordered five dozen wild boars, five dozen goats and as many fowls and birds that were available. They ordered three dozen bags of guinea corn to be grounded into flour to make their traditional food. Kufuo didn't worry too much about the refreshments because he knew that his guests would provide these on the day.

Preparations for the wedding reached a frenzied pitch. Soon, the day of the wedding was upon them. The drums and the Abeng horns welcomed the dawn, they announced the wedding that was about to take place. The Junkanoo bands dressed in their animal masks, stilts and colourful dress played the drums. They paraded around the outskirts of Cotts Hall welcoming their guests. The planters wondered at the noise. The majestic Africans dressed in their finest attire climbed the bumpy pathways to Cotts Hall. The hillsides were full of gaily-dressed folk going to an African wedding.

Before long the ceremonial stools were placed under an enormous Guango tree, the elders and chief took their seats. They wore robes slung over their shoulders in the style of the Ashanti chiefs of Ghana. The women took their places next to the chiefs and elders. I, Anancy, addressed the elders and blessed the wedding parties. I placed two more stools made of animal skins in the centre of the gathering. I invited the elders to start the ceremony. Simultaneously, a male and female elder brought the couple to the marriage stools.

Esi was dressed in a deep yellow and a purple robe with headdress to match and a pair of earring made from local metals. They were placed on the stools next to each other. Kufuo wore traditional African warrior dress with a loincloth of the best quality animal skin. A crown of feathers, a leather sash with a sheath and dagger were placed across his shoulders. Kufuo the African warrior who was willing to die to protect his animals, as well as his people.

The sounds of the horns and drums marked the beginning of the ceremony. The elders blessed the ground on which they were gathered. They blessed the couple and called on the ancestors along with the forces in the spirit world, to guide and give them many children. They sprinkled blessed water on them and spoke in numerous languages, to accommodate their guests from across the continent. Then, they were pronounced man and wife, according to the traditions of their motherland. I, Anancy, placed the two decorated broom handles on the ground and hand in hand Esi and Kufuo walked over them, signifying a new start and future for them. The couple exchanged food and their union was sealed.

The ceremony over the festivities began. The guests danced, ate and sang for two whole days. They forgot about the forty-five hours of apprenticeships down the hillsides for the time being. The married couple went back to their village. They had to work out how to spend the little money left over, after their enormous and memorable African wedding. Next day, as they sorted through their bridal bags they found their wedding gifts. They found a small bag of Maccaronys, small coins valuing about one shilling and a few guinea pieces. They were grateful for them for they would be able to begin the search, for a relatively small piece of land to lease, rent, or buy with their tiny deposit.

CHAPTER 11

The smallest of plots

The happy couple were delighted with their wedding gift. It was a small bag of coins; that would be enough for a deposit on a piece of land if they could find land at a price they could afford. The planters had stolen the fertile and flat land for their plantations. They had made sure that the ambitious Africans would not be able to own land and definitely not fertile and productive land to compete with them. The hillsides were left empty because, as long as they were not occupied, they provided no hiding or resting places for runaway and aspiring Africans.

The neglected hillsides grew rich and fertile waiting for suitable tillers to reap their rewards. The hillsides, the pathway to freedom in the mountains for the enslaved Africans, had now become the routes to dignity and self-sufficiency in their quest for total control of their lives. The free Africans with their limited resources were impatient to move out of the sphere of the plantations, onto these sheltered hillsides and undulating land.

In the meantime, the planters were planning elaborate strategies to keep them in their cane pieces. Free Africans acquired hillside land, at prices they could afford until they could find more flat and fertile land at reasonable prices. Kufuo and Esi sought land and found a small piece of sloping land of about an eighth of an acre. It was unsuitable for large-scale cultivation, but their leftover money could stretch no further, and they accepted this. They were indeed fortunate to be free Africans and have a deposit to put down on a rocky piece of land. They were now in control of their destiny and future. They accepted the challenge of the stony and hilly slope. They agreed it was suitable for a relatively small animal pen.

They decided to grow ground provisions, vegetables and some fruits on the flattest part of the land. The pen would only take a few goats, a couple of pigs as well as a donkey. Kufuo could look after a horse or cow for an apprentice for a few coins each month. Their work roles were decided by the nature of the hillside plot, Kufuo the shepherd and Esi, the farmer. The couple discussed where they would build their house and chose a slightly elevated ridge which jutted out on one side of the plot.

The pair delayed constructing their new home for a few more months. First, they would have to work and save enough money to feed their friends and family, who would help them build their home over two or three days. The couple left the sloping plot and set out for the mission, to earn enough money to buy building materials and food to feed their extended family of builders.

Esi arranged the foodstuff as well as the women who would help her cook for a small army of builders. Kufuo paid the bills and collected the necessary materials. On the appointed Saturday and Sunday, some Africans including Osei left the plantations and went to the hillside plot. Free Africans also went to the plot. They were given bowls of steaming corn meal porridge flavoured with cinnamon, spices and sweetened with molasses. At the end of the meal, the men and women moved ahead and attacked the hillside to carve out a foundation. The women collected the bowls and carried stones to lay the foundation for the house.

Next, they moved to a clearing to build the largest fire they could make. Esi had secured a petite wild boar for lunch, along with yams and sweet potatoes to be washed down with a drink made of molasses, water and lime juice. A roasting platform was built above the fire, the wild pig was placed on top of it, as it cooked a couple of the women scraped off the thick hairy skin, now dislodged by the heat. They turned it over and over until the juices ran out to show it was ready. The delicious smell of the roasting boar and the freshly roasted ground provisions encouraged the men to stop work and eat.

The women watched in dismay as almost all the meat on the animal disappeared in a short time, leaving only scant pieces of flesh on the carcass. They vowed that they would not get the leftovers next time. Kufuo spoke to Esi before returning to the building plot. He told her that they all expected the cooks to be the first to taste and eat the delicious meals, that they had prepared. He was insisting on half a goat at the next meal. Anticipating the excellent meal that they knew were being cooked for them, the men worked quickly and steadily to build the foundations. They piled medium sized stones on top of each other until they met on the other side. Then sand and thick clay soil were placed on them, and larger stones were placed on top. The cycle continued until the sun travelled across the sky indicating dusk and another mealtime.

The women had learnt their lesson. They rekindled the fire under the spit and laid a seasoned medium sized goat on it. They grounded freshly harvested maize and stirred it into coconut milk, turning it until all the liquid was absorbed by the corn. They covered it and left it to gently steam. The chefs told the men that the meal would be ready in an hour or so. They cut the goat in half and scooped out some turned maize meal into their bowls. The ladies cut generous amounts of the goat and ate until they were full. Afterwards, they ate some of the delicious fruits they had brought with them. As soon as, they had finished eating, they heard the men coming towards their makeshift kitchen.

Hurriedly, they placed the bowls of steaming turned maize meal and pieces of the goat meat in front of them. The men ate greedily, not noticing the missing half of the goat. Finishing their meal, the builders retired to the cool of the Silk Cotton tree to serve themselves some potent refreshments. The men drank for most of the night; they talked about the changes that were taking place and the best ways to make use of them. The well fed workers talked and talked until one by one they fell asleep under the extensive branches of the tree.

The women took shelter in the half-built house and slept soundly. They woke at the crack of dawn and prepared the breakfast. The cooks made an enormous pot of soursop leaf tea to wash away the excess of the men's hangover, served with roasted cassava dumplings and Callaloo. The women ate first. The cycle continued the following day with the women preparing a range of enjoyable meals and then they fetched stones to complete the house. On the third day, Kufuo and Esi were left to finish the house by covering the roof with dried tree branches woven into sturdy bamboo poles.

The couple were now alone in their two-roomed stone house with a room for themselves and one for their animals. Their new life was about to begin, each one with their well-defined area of expertise.

CHAPTER 12

The great
plantation collapse

The plantations had been there for an eternity, it seemed as if they would be there forever. The planters and their government imagined and saw them as etched into the landscape, of the islands and the mainland that they had enslaved. After 1807, the Backra had prayed for a never-ending supply of African labour at rock bottom prices. They hoped that the competition between the slave traders would push down prices. Passionately, they also prayed that the Negro women would breed abundantly for the survival of their cane pieces. The slave masters visualised their children or heirs carrying on the great work they had started. They would inherit their estates with their great houses. It was a life they imagined would never cease and they did not want to, or would allow it to end.

If the planters and their government fantasised about the continuation of their plantations, the former slaves now designated Apprentices visualised their rapid escape from them. They envisaged a swift and speedy end to the apprenticeships and their extended enslavement. In their frustration and anger at their plight, they seized on one of the clauses that Parliament had been forced to incorporate into the 1833 Act. It allowed them to buy their freedom. The planters had fought ferociously against the inclusion of this clause in the Act. They feared the existence of this clause deep in their hearts. They knew that their industrious and hard working apprentices would take advantage of it to buy their freedom, thus destroying their plantations, sources of income and, therefore, their control over them.

The Backra had watched as their slaves in their few hours away from their cane pieces, grow crops on their miniature and rock strewn house plots, provision grounds and traded profitably in the Sunday markets. They knew that their Negroes were saving money, they feared for the survival of their plantations and themselves.

The conscientious and hard-working apprentices, who could afford it, bought their way out of slavery as soon as they could by working on their small plots and saving together. They continued to challenge forcefully and deeply resented the apprenticeship system. They sabotaged the sugar growing processes to end their enslavement.

Infuriated, at the loss of their total control over the labour of the apprentices, the agents and overseers used every opportunity to wring every ounce of work out of them. They complained that they were working too slowly. They were taking too long to walk to the cane pieces as well as taking too long to eat their meagre lunches. They whined that the Act had made their apprentices idle as well as defiant. They would make them work twice as hard to make up for the many hours the Act had stolen from them. The overseers increased their scrutiny of the apprentices. They intensified their cocktail of punishments to force them to work harder and faster. Powerless to stop the exodus, the planters ordered more whipping and shackling of some of the apprentices, to frighten the others to increase their production.

Each morning, some cane piece workers were placed in the stocks with iron masks over their faces, and they were brutally beaten. Some were tied to the water troughs and flogged constantly. Others were chained to posts and left dangling in the hot sun for days. The punishments became more sadistic as the overseers tried to extract the maximum work from them. Daily, the house of correction in the plantation yards, bulged with enslaved Africans. The huge wheels of the treadmill creaked and groaned under the weight of the male and female apprentices tied to its upper pole. Slowly, the wheels turned as the overseer's whip tore into their already swollen and blistered flesh, inwardly

A drawing of slaves being punished on the treadmill in the House of Correction on a Jamaican plantation. Image reference NW0196. Source: www.slaveimages.org. Sponsored by the Virginia Foundation for the Humanities and the University of Virginia Library. Courtesy of authors Jerome S. Handler and Michael L. Tuite Jr.

they moaned and wailed. This did not break their spirit of resistance, they merely plotted their revenge.

The planters asked why should they pay their apprentices to work the extra hours they needed when they would only use their wages to buy their way out of their plantations and ruin them? Infuriated at their dwindling authority over their apprentices, the Backra immersed themselves in drinking rum, gambling and abusing the African women on their plantations. At times, the planters gambled to enlarge their cane pieces or to win money to pay off their debts. They also tried very hard to forget that their much-needed workforce was dwindling; as the diligent apprentices eagerly and confidently bought their way out of slavery.

Many of the apprentices in the plantation houses were enraged at their continued enslavement. They felt that the Act should have freed them in 1834 because they were not field workers. They joined with the field apprentices to end their oppression. They informed them of the planters' every action, their wrongdoings and the dates of their gambling sessions. Together, they intended to strike the fatal blow to the planters, the apprenticeships and slavery. Again, they approached their senior Anancy, they begged him to be at the gambling table. They wanted him, once more, to take back an infinitesimal amount of the wages the Backra had stolen from them, and were still pocketing, by forcing them to work without pay for centuries.

The oldest Backra had continued to host the gambling sessions on his estate. The planters wanted to increase their incomes to protect them against the uncertain times and the declining production in their cane pieces. This Backra became more brutal towards his apprentices because the Act had reduced their hours of work. He would wrench every ounce of labour from them before 1840. Vigorously, the apprentices worked on their small plots in the mountains, to earn enough money to buy their freedom and escape their vindictive owner.

Some of them fled to the mountaintops as before while others put their hard earned money into Anancy's saving club, the Pardner. Armed with the information on the gambling sessions, Anancy was in the midst of the game. Night after night, he again secreted guineas from the card table onto his person. The planters squealed as their money disappeared in front of their eyes. After each game, they borrowed money to pay back their losses, but again they lost the money they had borrowed. Their debts mounted. Their creditors and families in England refused their requests for money to pay off their arrears.

Desperate, some planters offered their plantations to the moneylenders. They too refused; their skill was in lending money not running hazardous plantations. The plantations were of no use to them without the guaranteed free labour of the Africans forever. They demanded that the planters repay their debts, frightened of losing everything some sold off the stony parts of their plantations to pay them. The free as well as some enslaved apprentices pooled their money and bought these rocky pieces of land.

The Backra host had played the biggest trick of all on his fellow planters. He had rigged the games and had stolen money from the card table each time a game was played. His actions helped to cover up Anancy's removal of the guineas. The actions of the host and Anancy sealed the fate of his fellow planters. He was hoarding money to make sure his plantation would be functioning at the end of the apprenticeships.

The apprentices railed against the Backra host for viciously forcing them to increase sugarcane production in his cane piece. His cheating at the gambling table had made him feel more secure about his future; they plotted to get rid of the brute once and for all. Again, they spoke to Anancy and told him about their new plan, together they would inflict the final blow on this repugnant Backra. They would destroy him and his plantation and buy their freedom before the six years were up.

This time, they asked Anancy to take on a more substantial role. He would assume the rank of a wealthy and influential Backra planter. He would then be able to play openly at the card table and win back more of the wages owed to them for their freedom fund. Anancy was delighted with the idea; he intended to strike the decisive blow against this malicious individual and plantation slavery. The host was delighted at the prospect of new blood and money. Briefly, he had wondered at this unknown planter in front of him, but his greed had stopped him from questioning or seeking too closely into his background.

They arranged to meet on his plantation on a breezy evening. A few of his fellow planters came along hoping to win back some guineas to get back their plantations. Anancy dressed in his finest morning suit, with a face that looked almost white and British, took his place at the card table. Diligently, the house apprentices attended their master; he must not suspect a thing. As they poured rum into their goblets, they drank with passion. The wealthy planter requested some of the ruby red drink that the Africans had placed next to the cask of rum. He explained to his fellow Backra that he had got quite accustomed to this delicious drink, that his apprentices made on his plantation at this time of the year. Anancy bragged that his goblet had as much rum as they had in theirs but, fortunately, his drink was slow to induce drunkenness. He told them that he always tried to stay sober when playing. He invited his host and the other planters to try the delicious ruby red drink. They apologised and begged to continue with the drink that gave them the most pleasure, rum.

The desperate planters placed their bets and money, but their host had again rigged the game in his favour. The host and the wealthy planter continued playing. Secretly, the other players wished he would lose everything because they suspected that he had cheated them, but they had no proof. The very wealthy planter and the host played game after game. Pleased with himself the host called an end to the session, he had won all but two of the games.

Nervously, the wealthy planter pleaded with him to let him have one last chance, to win back a little money to pay his agent and overseer. He also needed money to buy his apprentices their monthly rations of guinea corn and salted beef. Gleefully the host agreed; he was happy to take every guinea from this very wealthy but stupid planter who did not know when to stop playing.

The game began, and the prosperous plantation owner lost the first game. The host wanted to finish the game so he could count all the money; he had won on this very eventful night. Almost in tears, the previously wealthy planter begged to bet the last ten guineas, which had somehow hidden themselves in the folds of his breeches. Chuckling, the host agreed. Confidently, he sorted and arranged his cards; he placed all the money he had won including his saving on the card table. Impatiently, he looked about the room for the game to be over.

Slowly, and deliberately, the formerly wealthy planter placed his cards on the table. One by one the swindled Backra gasped. A little perturbed by the reaction of his fellow players, the host looked again at his cards. Anguish and misery spread across his cratered and sadistic face. The very wealthy planter had won the last game and all his money including his savings. He seethed, raged, pleaded and crawled on his hands and knees to the exceedingly wealthy planter. He asked him for another game to win back some of his losses. He said he would do anything he wanted. He begged to be told what he could do to please him and win back a few guineas to feed what he called his poor, poor apprentices.

Disdainfully, the super wealthy planter told him it was late, they needed their rest. He might return the following week if he was not indisposed to play another game. The wretched Backra fell on his knees and kissed Anancy's hairy hands. He offered to send him the best fruits, as well as the most beautiful African women on his plantation for his enjoyment. Angrily, the exceedingly wealthy planter declined his offer and left.

When the very wealthy planter had left, he shooed everyone out of his house and off his plantation. He opened another cask of rum and poured himself goblet after goblet. At sunrise, the house apprentices found him slumped over the container of rum. His face and hair were immersed in it. Soon the news spread, the enslaved Africans dropped everything and came to see the dying brute. They looked at him with scorn and delight. Gleefully, they left him to drown in the commodity, he and the other planters had used to enslave and exploit them over the centuries.

Before long the moneylenders arrived, they searched his house for the money he owed them. They found none, so they applied to the magistrates to have the plantation sold to pay his debts. As all the planters had hefty debts, they were reluctant to risk their money, buying a cane piece without apprentices. The moneylenders would not lend them any more money. The agent was forced to cut up the plantation into small plots. The apprentices seized their opportunity. They used their savings from the Pardner and Anancy's compensation fund from the poker game to buy their freedom and small plots to farm collectively on the plantation of the planter who had brutalised them daily without mercy.

Many plantations lay in ruin as the apprentices left. Sugar prices also fell as sugar beet replaced sugarcane in Europe, to sweeten the much-loved tea of the British people stolen from China. Desperate, the British government abolished the apprenticeships two years before they were due to end.

Finally, the rebellious and resourceful Africans on the plantations on the islands and the mainland had freed themselves. They were victorious over the violence, brutality and inhumanity of plantation slavery which had disfigured and distorted the islands and the mainland for over three hundred years.

CHAPTER 13

Emancipation

The conscientious and jubilant Africans, led by their loyal and versatile senior Anancy, fled from the sugar plantations. They were determined that they would never enter them again; as they flung off the visible and invisible chains and shackles, which had restricted their freedom, human dignity and craving for self-determination for centuries. Men, women and children colonised the surrounding hillsides and undulating lands that the planters had scorned for their unproductiveness. These virgin lands held no horrific memories for them, only honesty and the potential to restore their human dignity through the honest and noble cultivation of the God-given earth. These bare slopes welcomed them. These hilly inclines had been their route to another life in the mountains away from plantation slavery. Now, this same dense virgin soil, with rocks beneath the meagre vegetation, would again be their lifeline, away from the plantations.

The liberated Africans inhaled the mustiness and aroma of the semi-dry earth. They visualised the constant crops sprouting from this once uncultivated but fertile land. They tasted and savoured the future of the hillsides and the rippling ground. They bought, rented, leased or squatted on the earth to reclaim their independence and human dignity. The farmers delved into the bare but partially fertile hillsides around them. The hillsides blossomed with small compact settlements dotted on the hilly elevations. Production increased fast and ferociously, as the Africans made up for the stolen centuries of crop growing dictated by the planters' profit, sugar cultivation.

The privacy and seclusion of the hillsides allowed them to reproduce naturally. They sought to rebuild their family relationships and structures which would sustain them in freedom. They revived the agriculture of their motherland and also drew on the natural vegetation of the islands, as well as many of the farming practices of the original peoples of the islands and the mainland. The hillsides fulfilled the fledgeling farmers' faith in Mother Nature. The hillsides did not disappoint, yams, dasheen, cassava and sweet potatoes snuggled beneath the soil. They grew happily until it was time to be harvested consumed and sold in the flourishing Sunday markets.

The meticulous African farmers looked after their crops tenderly and topped up the hillsides with soil and manure, but most of all, with love. They reinstated, valued and appreciated the cooperative relationship which had developed between themselves and the soil between the rocky hillsides. Once the farmers had secured their daily bread, they looked inquisitively at their hillside mounds to see what cash crops could be gotten from them to provide the essentials they did not have. The miniature farms on the hilly peaks diversified producing a range of foods and other products. These included cotton, logwood, logwood extract dye and cedar wood for export. They also grew, consumed and sold coffee, turmeric, thyme, peppers, peanuts, pumpkins, arrowroot, pimento, ginger, melons and oil nut(castor oil). They cultivated as many small crops as they could sell to provide an income to improve their lives.

In the corner of their smallholdings, they made coops that held chickens and ducks. The steeper heights provided grazing for goats, donkeys, pigs, cows, to supplement their incomes. The resilient Africans were fulfilling their destiny. Their enterprise would grow as the sugar and coffee plantations starved of their free labour declined naturally. The grasping planters did not want to and always refused to pay the correct value for human work. Many plantations fell into ruin so nature reclaimed the land.

The newly imported indentured servants from, China, India and Madeira, laboured relentlessly after 1838. However, they

Current map of the parishes and parish capitals of Jamaica. Adapted from caribbeanexams.com

were unable to revive the large-scale sugar plantations which were built on the blood and sacrifice of, first, the Taino and Amerindian peoples, and then the Africans. The Africans' yearning for flat and fertile land was always threatened by the new planters, the banana companies from North America. They intended to make this exquisite and bountiful island one colossal banana plantation after 1838, with the liberated Africans as wage slaves. Banana companies, such as the United Fruit Company, had acquired a significant number of the abandoned sugar plantations. Banana became the new King on the island.

However, the majority of the ambitious African farmers and their relations turned their backs on this new form of wage slavery. They seized the opportunity to acquire the land that they and their ancestors had laboured on relentlessly for three centuries or more. They knew it was the only dignified way of securing an income for themselves and their families from their liberation onwards. The planters had been compensated for freeing the Africans. The Africans had not been compensated. Many determined African women and men had bought their freedom thus creating more wealth for the planters.

The result of the European invasion of the islands and the mainland was that the indigenous peoples were near to extinction. Millions of Africans had been callously worked to death on the plantations, and millions more had died needlessly on their way to the islands. However, they had destroyed slavery.

Keeping with their past practices local and colonial governments washed their hands of the enduring Africans. They left them to find their own schools, housing, healthcare and transport. Willingly, the ingenious Africans accepted the challenge. They grabbed the opportunity when they could to escape from the hilly peaks to the flat and fertile lands of the plantations, now exhausted by sugar and coffee growing for centuries. They would revive these flat and formerly fertile lands. They moved onto the abandoned sugar plantations when they had enough money to buy a small plot. African production grew and grew; soon they became the chief producers of goods for export on the island. Their only rivals were the well-financed banana companies from North America and the remaining solvent planters.

Kufuo sold his hillside plot to Osei, his herding partner from Akin at an affordable price. Osei was delighted; he would continue the good work of his herding partner from Akin until he could buy more flat and fertile land. Kufuo acquired a flat piece of land in a nearby parish, where the plantation collapse was most severe, and the prices were negotiable. The bankrupt sugar plantation was so vast it would take years for the planter's agent to sell the plots. This gave Kufuo as well as the liberated Africans time to extend their acreage when they could afford it.

Sisi and Jaimimi ran along the track towards their new home. They had loved roaming between the animal pen and the vegetable plot of their hillside home. Now, they had outgrown it and sought new adventures.

"Where is the mill?" Jaimimi asked impatiently.

"Patience is a virtue," replied Esi.

"You will know when we get there," Kufuo answered.

The children walked beside their parents on the narrow dirt track, impatient to reach their destination and their new home.

"It's there, isn't it? It's the mill with the horse going around and around," pointed and screamed Sisi.

"This is our new home. I was very lucky to get the mill and the cane piece in the distance. We have enough land to make an animal pen, grow provisions, cash crops such as sugarcane, coffee, ginger, pimento, cedar and logwood as well as fruits. We have loads of space to improve that imposing old and creaky wooden house to take our family and friends," he told his family proudly.

"You won't be playing anymore, there will be work in the fields, as well as schooling from morning to night for you both," Esi informed them.

At first light, the children were out in the yard stroking the horses as they went around and around turning the mill. The cane juice oozed from the factory into the zinc funnel and then into the boiling house to be reduced to sugar crystals and molasses.

"Last one to the coffee bushes is a donkey," Sisi dared her brother.

The children picked the ripe coffee beans from the small bushes, filling their little sacks as they moved along the rows. Next, the workers and the children poured the coffee beans onto the huge raised platform on wheels (roll-in) to dry in the sun. Every evening, they pushed the beans on the roll-in under the sprawling wooden house on stilts to keep them dry. Before going to bed, the children walked around the pen stroking and bidding the work animals good night.

The tropical fruit trees provided both nourishment and a play space for the children and their friends. They had a ready supply of lunches and snacks giving their parents the space they needed to get a living from their varied plots. In the cane pieces among the cane, they grew yams, dasheen, cassava and other produce to supplement their meals.

Sisi and Jaimimi attended Sunday school at the local Moravian church, as well as reading and writing classes during the week. Esi wanted her children to be farmers. She also had aspirations for them to enter the emerging professions for a liberated people, if they were so inclined. Kufuo's home became the centre of village life, the small farmers used the mill to crush the cane and boil it into sugar. Kufuo continued to expand his plot to provide the communal services the developing African community needed. He and his family were established in a free and thriving African village.

CHAPTER 14

The African revival

The Africans' pent-up potential exploded after liberation in 1838. Two years before the British government's timetable for the end of the apprenticeships. The obstinate Africans had worn them down. The Africans' dormant abilities and enterprise were renewed, these diversified and strengthened as the planters and their government gave in and left them to control their destiny for the time being. If they had exploited their labour ruthlessly during slavery, why would they bother with them now that they had fought them and won their freedom? They provided for themselves. The years of servitude as an enslaved workforce, and then as unpaid apprenticed labour, had prepared them for the task of creating the services they needed on a daily basis.

They drew on their natural abilities, the knowledge embedded in their African personality, their ancient civilisations and the wisdom the first peoples of the islands and the mainland had shared with them. The exodus from the plantations fuelled a boom in small villages and market towns across the island. Now, the Africans' limitless and innate abilities were unleashed. Cottage industries mushroomed; everyone was and could be master of his or her own destiny. Small village centres sprang up as the proactive Africans used the crafts they had so skilfully learnt during slavery and for which they had not been paid. They refined and expanded them to provide services for their new communities and their fellow Africans.

The small fishing fleet from Bax Hall established itself further along the coast. The fishing fleet began to grow. Parents encouraged their sons to join the fleet. Their apprenticeships were comprehensive; they dug out the massive fallen trunks of the Guango and Silk Cotton trees and made them into fishing boats. They sailed the coast with a captain and learnt their craft. The island's fishing fleet was born. Now, they supplied each other with a variety of fresh fish and seafood. The entrepreneurial skills of the African masses were let loose.

The liberated Africans could not afford the imported goods made in the factories of Britain. Why should Africans maintain the economy of the very system that had stolen the proceeds of their labour, over the centuries and dehumanised and violated their humanity? The money they got from their plots had to be used for their and their community's benefit and development. They used the local resources and their skills to create and fashion the local industries they needed. The demand for goods and services outstripped the small family production in the compounds. The tiny potter's yard attracted young men and women to fashion pots and storage jars for water and grain, their apprenticeships were comprehensive and rewarding. They catered for the growing business and home use across the villages, towns and parishes of the island. The imported goods from Britain remained unsold.

The blacksmiths provided genuine apprenticeships to skill the young people unable to work the land. They made shoes for the horses to journey across the island for trade and recreation. The zealous African masses worked the land intensively and needed tools to till fertile as well as unfertile soil. Modest agricultural tools became their chief output. Those who could not afford to buy or lease land purchased food from the aspiring farmers and sold it in the villages and towns. At dusk, these higglers and traders prepared the leftovers and sold the foodstuff to travellers and those without the means to cook for themselves. The majority of the liberated Africans farmed the land, and this became their primary source of income.

The tropical climate guaranteed constant sunshine, outdoor living and working. It also caused illnesses which were often the result of their back-breaking work and their everyday practices.

Frequently, they were in need of medical assistance. Naturally, they drew on the medicines that the medicine people had refined and perfected in their homelands and then during slavery. Daily, children were born and were attended to by medical practitioners and midwives, medical services were available. The skills of the traditional medicine people flourished and surpassed that of the European-trained doctors, as their elders used the remedies they had developed. These medicines were often so powerful in curing illnesses that they had become acceptable on the plantations. Grudgingly, they appeared on the estates' records as used by Negro doctors. Many of the natural remedies employed to cure fever and diseases were first used by African herbal specialists and the Obeah women and men on the plantations during slavery.

In Kingston, the future capital of the island, a young girl of European and African parentage watched her mother grow and mix herbs and plants. She used the herbs to heal the sick and dying soldiers of the British Army who visited her father. Dutifully, she helped her mother mix and administer the herbal medicines to the frequently sick and dying soldiers, as well as the Backra on the island. Hourly, British soldiers, officials and their families were dying from many diseases. Her parents' home became a miniature hospital, where the military and the local people came in search of medicines to treat their illnesses.

As you would expect, over time her knowledge of plants and herbs and their uses to treat a range of diseases were enhanced. She had been a willing apprentice to her mother, and she learnt her craft thoroughly. Eager to improve her practice she visited many islands and two countries on the mainland, where men from the islands were working in the most appalling conditions. The building of the Panama railway gave her the opportunity to practice the skills she had so carefully learnt from her mother. The company had recruited thousands of workers from the islands. The largest number came from her homeland, Jamaica.

These men had worked in the most atrocious conditions for a minuscule wage and almost no medical provisions. Thousands of workers had died before the railroad was completed. Those who returned to the island told of the terrible working conditions there. The labourers also spoke about the illnesses that were rife in the steamy jungles of Panama, such as cholera, malaria, yellow fever, dysentery and much more. They needed medical attention.

In 1851, Mary Seacole went to Panama where she was able to use her knowledge of herbs and plants, to help her fellow Africans, as well as the other imported workers. At the same time, she took every opportunity to acquire more knowledge of the plants and herbs used by the indigenous peoples of Panama and, as a result, she expanded her existing medical knowledge and skills. Not satisfied with the skills she had learnt in Panama, she went on to the banana plantations of Costa Rica. In Costa Rica, very little or no medical services were available for the hundreds of migrant labourers from Jamaica, the other islands and elsewhere. Again, she was able to practice her skills in treating the sick and, at the same time, her knowledge and competence in treating a range of illnesses were improved.

By the time she arrived and volunteered to help the sick and wounded soldiers in the Crimean War in 1854, she was a skilled and experienced practitioner with many, many years in the medical profession. Her offer of help was refused by Florence Nightingale and the British war office, so she set up the British Hotel in the Crimea, where she treated wounded British soldiers. They greatly appreciated her commitment and devoted assistance to them. She not only treated their physical illnesses but comforted and listened to their 'worries'. This was a great comfort to them and helped them to recover. Years later, they remembered and honoured her for caring for them.

Mary Seacole was an accomplished and knowledgeable medical practitioner when she arrived in Europe. The conditions in her homeland and on the mainland had given her the most rigorous training for her future work. She had made treating the sick her profession. She devoted her life to improving the health of the sick where ever it was needed, whether it was in the islands, on the mainland or in Europe.

Education was also a burning issue for the liberated Africans during slavery and after their emancipation. The planters' learning appeared to give them power over them. Many intelligent and studious Africans craved it as a means of improving their future. Liberation gave them the opportunity to acquire some of this learning and they embraced it willingly. Those accompanying the planters to church, Sunday after Sunday, had listened and learnt the words written in the planters' holy book that they prized and valued. Secretly, they had passed this learning on to their families in the battle to end slavery. Passing on learning to family members, colleagues and neighbours became an integral part of the development of the African Diaspora, after emancipation and beyond in the islands and the mainland.

Later, these scholarly individuals set up small places of learning to pass on the skills of reading and writing to those who wanted it and could afford the tiny fees. From these modest sites of learning, gradually, a system of primary schooling was established, again with help from the Moravian and Baptist churches and philanthropists. It wasn't until the turn of the century that the colonial government, again had to be forced to provide schooling for a minuscule number of scholarly Africans.

As early as 1722, the Bax family, from Bax Hall plantation, had donated money to set up a school for the children of the poor whites in the surrounding parishes. Their aim was to prepare them for the minor jobs on the plantations, as well as in the colonial administration. The school was first set up in the Parish of St Ann, but later it moved to the new capital of the island after emancipation. Much later it became Jamaica College. Over time, these elite institutions were forced to enrol many inquisitive and gifted Africans. In these institutions, they demonstrated their natural intelligence convincingly.

The Africans were not insulated from the planters' religion in 'The Enslaved World', although they were banned from taking part in it until it suited them and their government. In contrast, the non-conformist churches such as the Moravians and Baptists had challenged slavery from the beginning. They saw the institution of slavery as impinging on their mission, to win the hearts and souls of the Africans for their God and denomination. These missionaries had to save the Africans from the darkness of their traditional ancestor worship, as well as their reverence and guardianship of all things in nature big and small. They had to be weaned off worshiping the elements that gave them life, like the sun that warmed them and brought forth food on the land. They had to be stopped from praising and respecting the Gods of their motherland, who had sustained them throughout their time in the sweltering cane pieces when the overseers' whips ate into their bare flesh. These crusaders were fanatical in bringing the Africans into the Christian fold, to civilise and control them for their God.

The Africans were now free, and their worship reflected their freedom. Slavery had trained the African in the art of survival, as well as giving them an acute appreciation of justice, and those who had demonstrated it in their relations with them. The spiritual, as well as the religious practices of Africa, had been asleep inside their souls waiting to come out. They could and would not put aside what had made them Africans. Practically, they fused some of their African Gods and religious practices with some of the rituals and symbols of the non-conformist churches, in particular, the Baptist church.

The African lay preachers of this faith had fuelled the resistance of the Africans against the planters' necessity, to keep them on the plantations forever. As liberated Africans, they created the religious forms which embodied the essence of their African culture. Their worship contrasted with the grimness and stiffness of the planters. African religious observances consumed the whole body, the mind and spirit. Their trance-like states and quivering movements were a testimony that they were possessed, with the spirits of their ancestors. Religious spaces were the central meeting places outside their workplaces, to revive and celebrate their unbroken relationship with their fore-parents, motherland and with each other.

In their worship and collective practices, the ancestors spoke to them. They transcended their bodies and language as well as feats to levels only they could know and appreciate. The centuries of longing and hope were realised in their spiritual and religious worship; as well as the dance of freedom. They incorporated the instruments so dear to them, such as the drums, Abeng horns and conch shells.

The Africans had abolished slavery and the plantation system, which they had resisted for more than three centuries because they were a strong and determined people. The liberated Africans would live the only way they knew, they would live as autonomous and self-directing Africans, away from their ancestral homes in Africa.

CHAPTER 15

The dance of freedom

The Africans fled from the plantations to the rocky hillsides and irregular landscape of the islands and the mainland. They were determined to transform and banish forever the brutality of plantation slavery, that had been inflicted on the natural and civilised world for more than three hundred years. They seized the chance to recreate, balance and link all aspects of their African personality to the sounds, rhythms, spirituality and creativity of Africa's ancient civilisations.

The liberation revelry gave way to the traditional end of year Christmas celebrations. The rhythms and sounds of Africa exploded and seeped into their daily lives on the hillsides. If the enslaved Africans had sung and hummed songs of freedom in the cane pieces, in freedom their every action and every thought revived, recalled and celebrated the traditional practices they could remember or half-remember.

Their voices perfected in the cane pieces bellowed out onto the hillsides. They caught the harmony of their fellow Africans tilling the soil. They sang and danced in honour of their hard-won freedom. They were thankful for the generosity of nature, their snake God Obi, the spirits of Africa and their ancestors who had guided them throughout their imprisonment in the cane pieces. Their joyfulness flavoured their actions and performances. Converging on the old meeting places under the Guango trees, the Junkanoo players, their senior Anancy and the liberated Africans rejoiced at their defeat of slavery.

The drums beat, the whistling and hollering drew everyone in, and the celebration and dance of freedom began. They danced the dance of freedom. I, Anancy, led the dance, the beat of the drums oozed into our bones, minds, souls and our very core. Our limbs spun, jumped and vibrated excitedly in our freedom dance. Water ran from our fatigued torsos, but freedom was precious, and so we danced beyond exhaustion to honour this supreme achievement. The girls and boys wheeled to the frantic beating of drums, conch shells and finger instruments crafted out of wood and metal. The elaborate masked animal faces of the Junkanoo players threatened the crowds, with their steadfast and menacing fierceness. The same fierceness that had won the victorious Africans the freedom they were now celebrating.

The elongated legs of the Junkanoo dancers manoeuvred expertly above the heads of the seated audience, in pursuit of the fleeing planters. Planters who were now in poverty, as the Africans' flight from their plantations had brought them to their knees, forcing them to chop up parts of their estates and sell it to those they had enslaved. The matrons hollered and shook their hips to the frenzied beating of the drums, as they had done as girls in their motherland and which had been interrupted in time. Now, as free women, they remembered and sharpened their movements surrounded by eager young girls replicating the skill of their dancing.

Then, the African warriors took to the stage; it was centuries since they were able to freely show off their skill in hunting and protecting their family members. They had revived these talents as they hunted among the dense terrain of the hillsides and mountainous regions of the island, which were now their homes, providing the basics for their survival in freedom. The delicacy of their catch, the boar's flesh, would one day become a national treat. The animated audience waited on the edge of the makeshift seats for the actions of the warriors. The thrill of the hunt and the defeat they had dreamt of in every generation, since the beginning of their enslavement. The Abeng horns blew loud and menacing in the planters' ears. In front of their eyes, they saw the scrawny corseted legs of the slave masters running for their lives. The planters were very thankful for the colonial army with its ammunition, muskets and cannons. They had ensured their vicious control of the Africans for centuries.

The menacing masks of the African warriors flung their hefty spears and daggers at the soldiers. The soldiers responded with their muskets and cannon fire. The iron balls of the cannons like magic flew into the air to the delight of the spectators. The power of the Obeah, medicine people and their senior Anancy had deflected the power of the planters. The Backra raged at the cowardice of their army and faced the warriors. Now confident and sure of their power, the masked group terrorised the planters that had enslaved them. The slave masters fled in a panic, the audience rejoiced at the sight. They begged for more. The thunderous drumming drew in the energetic Africans, honouring the freedom that they had wrenched from the planters and their government.

They danced the dance of freedom, fast, frenzied and systematic movements that gave way to leaping, swirling, twisting, as well as rolling until their bodies folded with exhaustion. Quickly, they were replaced by eager, young, vibrating bodies expressing their joy, while aiming to out-dance those that went before. As they wilted onto the solid earth, the drumbeats accelerated. Revived by the beat, they danced, again and again, the dance of freedom until they could dance no more. The drums grew silent, heralding the rising sun and a new day to craft, construct and combine their profound humanity with the legacy of their servitude under slavery.

The spirits of the ancestors entered the celebration of all celebrations and led the way. Women and girls wrapped in white from head to toe entered the arena. They swayed from side to side and pivoted in front of the audience until their bodies doubled over and hung motionlessly. They mouthed unfamiliar syllables to the thrilled revellers; they revived and paraded as one by one the spirits of the ancestors entered them. They shouted in tongues unknown to their audience. Collective hysteria overtook them, as they whirled, reeled and rotated before prostrating themselves onto the soil. Unashamedly, they flaunted their submission to the spirits of their ancestors, their Gods and the forces of the natural world around them. Finally, the life force re-entered their bodies and they revived and shook breathlessly, as the spirits of their ancestors bade them dance in praise of their liberation and deliverance. The perceptive Africans around them understood the signal. They awoke as the spirits penetrated their willing souls and bodies, and together they danced the dance of freedom. They sang and danced in gratitude, allowing their bodies and voices to express their joyfulness at their emancipation.

In their victorious triumph against slavery, they would in freedom build up those cultural as well as monetary forms, within their control to lay the foundations for alternative models of human relations. The liberated Africans shunned the individualism of the planter class and their allies. They sought the collectivism, egalitarianism and traditionalism of their motherland instead.

They could not embrace a monetary and social system that had denied them their humanity, by enslaving them for over three centuries. This economic and social system had justified their enslavement by attempting to inject into their consciousness the most destructive views of their intellectual ability as well as their physical beauty. This monetary and social system had defined them negatively for three hundred years. Therefore, it could and would never meet their collective need to be the vibrant intellectual and physically beautiful people, which nature had crafted and given the most generous nature.

The Africans' experience had been distorted and deformed by slavery. Thus, the astute and aware Africans would attempt to construct a different society to the one that had enslaved them, allowing them to return to the humanity of their African past. Whenever the African was in total control of their life, they excelled in art, education, science, music, human relations, the natural world as well as sports. In these capacities, the African excelled because the planter class could not control activities instilled in his or her dynamic personality.

However, on a daily basis, the Africans would have to confront, continually, the structural as well as a financial racism crafted and embedded in the society in which they live. They would also have to challenge the discriminatory practices of an international monetary system and its institutions. A financial system and its organisations which perpetuate itself, by exploiting and controlling the resources of the world for the benefit of a minority. It continues to systematically exploit and use the resources of the world at minimal cost to itself, to maintain its wealth and power. The Africans' journey is not yet over.

TIMELINE

800BC	Africans traded with the ancient peoples of the Americas and the world. They left huge images of themselves on the South American mainland.
1324	The King of the Malian Empire visited Cairo and took a lot of gold with him. This caused the value of gold to fall in Egypt.
1325	Mansa Musa, King of Mali, visits Mecca with his slaves.
1424	Prince Henrique, the Navigator of Portugal, sends the first known expedition to Africa. He finds the African population cultivating their staple crops and living comfortably in their compounds and villages.
1430	Portugal joins in the Arab slave trade and develops sugar plantations on the West Coast of Africa.
1444	Ships off the West African coast returns to Portugal with 12 Africans. This was the first recorded auction of Africans by Europeans in Lagos, Portugal
1452	Pope Nicholas V gives his permission to enslave anyone who was not a Christian, Catholics.
1462	The Cabo Verde islands off the west coast of Africa is said to be Portugal's first major settlement in Africa, because of the Portuguese buildings of around this date.
1482	Portugal sets up the first European trading post in the Gold Coast, Elmina Fort, Ghana.
1488	Bartolomeu Dias, from Portugal, sails around the Southern tip of Africa, the Cape of Good Hope on his way to the Indies.
1492	Columbus ran aground on The Bahamas, Dominica and Cuba. Columbus also ran aground on Ayiti, he claimed it for Spain and called it Hispaniola. It is estimated that there were 80 million indigenous people in the Americas. It is also estimated that by 1592, only 10 million were left.
1493	In the Treaty of Tordesillas, Pope Alexander V1 settles the claims of Portugal and Spain to their so-called newly discovered lands. Portugal was given Brazil and rights on the West African coast. Spain was handed the islands and the mainland of South America.

1494	Columbus drifts onto Jamaica's North Coast and claims it for Spain. He calls the place where he landed New Seville.
1498	The Spanish colonise Trinidad.
1499	The Portuguese built Fort Jesus on the island city of Mombassa off the Kenyan coast. They begin to explore the East Coast of Africa.
1500	The first Spanish speaking African slaves are brought to Hispaniola from Spain.
1500-1600	Portugal dominates the slave trade.
1502	Puerto Rico colonised by the Spanish.
1509	The first Africans are brought to Jamaica from Hispaniola.
1521	There are records which suggest that there was a massive slave rebellion in Hispaniola.
1526	The first Africans are brought to North America at Pee Dee River from Hispaniola. Soon after they fled into the interior and joined the indigenous people.
1528	The first Africans are brought to Venezuela.
1532	African slaves in Coro Venezuela rebels and runs away into the mountains.
1534	Spanish Town is made the capital of Jamaica by the Spanish, their first major settlement was New Seville.
1552-53	An Enslaved African named Miguel Rey led a rebellion against slavery in Venezuela.
1573	Elizabeth I, of Britain, officially sanctions the transportation of enslaved Africans in British vessels.
1616	The Netherlands claims Berbice in Guyana.
1625	Britain captures Barbados and settles at Hole Town
1627	Dominica is claimed by France.
1628	There are records of enslaved Africans arriving in Canada.
1632	The Netherlands claims St Eustatius.
1650	The Dutch dominated the slave trade.
1650	Grenada is claimed by the French.
1652	The Netherlands establishes a trading post at the Cape of Good Hope (South Africa).
1655	The British take Jamaica from the Spanish. It is estimated that the island produced 80 million tonnes of sugar each year. The British Government is said to have earned £250 million in taxes each year. The Spanish and their African slaves fled to the hills and mountains to fight the British. Some fled to Cuba and Hispaniola and plotted to retake the island.

1665	The British slave traders built a fort in Jamaica to house slaves before they were sold and distributed to the other islands and the mainland. From 1713, the British supply the Spanish colonies with slaves.
1669	William Drax of Barbados buys land in Jamaica. He names his new plantation Drax Hall after his smaller plantation in Barbados.
1670	Louis XIV officially allows the trade in African slaves to the French colonies.
1672	Denmark occupied St Thomas.
1673	There is a massive slave uprising in Jamaica.
1692	There is a slave rebellion in Barbados. An earthquake hits Port Royal in Jamaica, it is the busiest trading area in the Caribbean. Port Royal is the domain of the pirates and buccaneers.
1697	A treaty gives the western part of Hispaniola to France, it is renamed, St Domingue.
1700-1807	Britain dominates the slave trade.
1701	There is a massive slave uprising in Antigua and also in 1831.
1712	Slave revolts in New York City, a British colony.
1713	The British slave traders supply the Spanish colonies with slaves, making them the biggest suppliers of Africans to 'The Recently Enslaved World'.
1718	Denmark claims St John.
1721	Enslaved Africans escape to the mountains of Venezuela to set up a free town.
1730	Captain Cudjoe is the leader of the Western Maroon in Jamaica.
1732	Nanny is the leader of the Eastern Maroons in Jamaica.
1733	Slaves took over St John and held the island for six months.
1734	Nanny Town is destroyed by the British in Eastern Jamaica.
1738	African slaves revolt in North and South Carolina in North America.
1739	The first Maroon War in Jamaica and a subsequent treaty with the British.
1741	There is a Negro uprising in New York a fledgeling British colony.
1743	Toussaint L'Ouverture is born on the Breda plantation in St Domingue.
1760	Tacky's Rebellion in Jamaica, the resistance lasted many months.
1761	Continued slave revolts in Western Jamaica.

1765-1793	Suriname's Maroon Wars.
1785 -1790	Dominica's first Maroon War.
1789	The French revolution begins.
1790	African slaves revolt in St Domingue.
1791	The revolution begins in St Domingue
1792	The Danish Government announces its intention to abolish the slave trade in Danish ships. It was not until 1803 that the slave trade was abolished by Denmark.
1793	Toussaint L'Ouverture raises a massive slave army and defeats the French army.
1793	Louis XVI is executed, and France becomes a Republic.
1794	Slavery is abolished in all the French colonies including St Domingue.
1794	British and Spanish troops capture Port-Au-Prince, St Domingue.
1795	There is a significant slave revolt in Venezuela led by an enslaved African named Jose Chirinos. There are major slave rebellions in Curacao, Dominica, Grenada and St Lucia. Fedon's rebellion in Grenada had lasted 15 months before it was put down by the British. The Second Maroon War in Jamaica, the Maroons were forced to sign a treaty.
1796	The Trelawney Town Maroons were shipped from Jamaica to Nova Scotia and later to Sierra Leone in West Africa.
1802	Napoleon sends an army to St Domingue and the other French colonies to re-enslave the Africans.
1804	Jean-Jacques Dessalines declares St Domingue an independent Republic he is crowned King James I of Haiti.
1807	British ships can no longer transport slaves. Britain abolishes the slave trade in her colonies. The British planters obtained enslaved Africans from the Dutch, French instead.
1807	Officially enslaved African women are forced to breed the next generation of children to work as slaves.
1809-1814	Dominica's second Maroon war.
1814	Demerara, Berbice and Essequibo were ceded to Britain. Britain paid the Dutch for this land.
1816	There is a famous slave rebellion in Barbados led by Bussa, a slave.
1816-17	Simon Bolivar of Venezuela defeated the Spanish Empire. The enslaved Africans are freed if they fight in Bolivar's army against the Spanish.

1819-20	Simon Bolivar unites the liberated Spanish colonies as Gran Columbia.
1823	There is a significant slave rebellion in Demerara, Guyana on the South American coast.
1825	The Great African Slave Revolt in Cuba.
1830-1832	There are significant slave uprisings in Antigua, Barbados, Cuba, Jamaica, Martinique, Tortola and St John.
1831	Nat Turner's Slave Revolt in Virginia.
1831-32	The Western or Christmas Rebellion is led by Deacon Sam Sharp in Jamaica.
1833	The Act of Abolition is passed by the British Parliament to end slavery in the British colonies.
1834	The Act of Abolition is implemented. Africans in Antigua are freed but continue to work in the cane pieces for a minuscule wage. The Act also extends slavery for a further six years for the majority of enslaved Africans, i.e. the Africans are re-enslaved as apprentices.
1834	The Marquis Sligo the governor of Jamaica, tell the freed Africans that 'you will be apprenticed to your former owners for a few years to fit you for freedom'. Cornwall Chronicle 2nd August 1834. However, he freed his slaves in 1834.
1834	Enslaved Africans in St Kitts, Demerara and Trinidad rebel at the theft of their freedom once more by the British government.
1835	The planters begin to receive compensation to free the Africans they had enslaved.
1838	The Enslaved Africans force the British government to free them. Slaves are freed in South Africa and Mauritius.
1845	Indian Indentured servants are brought to work on the sugar plantations in Guyana, Jamaica and Trinidad.
1850	Many Africans from the islands are recruited to build the Panama Railways.
1854	Chinese indentured servants are brought to work on the sugar plantations in Jamaica.
1887	Marcus Garvey was born in St Ann, Jamaica.
1902 -1920	There is a mass migration of African-Barbadian and Jamaicans to the USA.
1912- 1930	Many Africans from Jamaica were recruited by the United Fruit Company to work in the Banana industry in Cuba.
1914	Africans were recruited from the islands to build the Panama Canal, especially from Barbados.

1914	Marcus Garvey set up the Universal Negro Improvement Association.
1914	Many Africans are recruited to the mother country Britain to fight or support in the First World War.
1929	Marcus Garvey sets up the first political party in Jamaica.
1938	Major strikes in the Caribbean a hundred years after emancipation. The condition of workers worsened as wages were cut because of the economic depression which began in America. The descendants of the enslaved Africans demanded that the sugar lands be turned over to them as compensation (reparation) for the labour of their ancestors. They believed that the Queen of England at that time made this promise to them.
1939	Africans from the islands are recruited to fight in the Second World War in Europe.
1948	Empire Windrush left the Caribbean islands with 500 invited African workers. They were recruited by various government departments in Britain to rebuild the economy after Hitler's destruction of its major cities.

SELECT BIBLIOGRAPHY

Atkinson, Nadine 2001. CXE Lecture Series – History: Kingston: *The Jamaica Observer*

Barton, Paul 2002. The History of the African-Olmecs: www.Community.webtv.net/paul nubia empire

Beck, Sanderson 2006. Spanish Conquest 1492-1580 www.san beck.org html

Campbell, Horace 2007. *Rasta and Resistance: From Marcus Garvey to Walter Rodney.* Hertfordshire: Hansib Publications

Carey, Bev 2012. *The Maroon Story: The Authentic and Original History of the Maroons in the History of Jamaica 1490-1880*: Gordon Town, Kingston: Agouti Press

Coelho, Paulo 1981. *Akapwitchi Akaporo Armas e Escravos: Maputo, Mozambique*: Instituto Nacional do Livro e do Disco

Davidson, Marcia 2003. Anancy Introduction: Jamaicans.com online

Eisner, Gisela 1961. *Jamaica 1830-1930: A Study in Economic Growth.* Manchester: Manchester University Press

Espeut, Peter 2003. Our Taino Heritage: Kingston *The Jamaica Gleaner*

Fraser, Sara 2003. *A Bitter Legacy New York*: NY, Severn House Publishers

Harris, Roxy 1979. *Caribbean English and Adult Literacy*: London: The Adult Literacy Unit

Hart, Richard 1989. *The Abolition of Slavery: Caribbean Labour Solidarity*: London, Karia Press

Jacobs, Curtis, 2002. The Fedons of Grenada 1763-1814 Conference Papers: www.openuwi.edu

JNHT 2005. Draxhall Water Wheel: Kingston JNHT Trust

JNHT 2011. Taino Verses Arawak: Taino Day: Kingston: JNHT Trust

Lewis, Matthew 1999. *Journal of a West India Proprietor*: Oxford, Oxford University Press

McFarlane, M 1977. *Cudjoe of the Maroon*; London, Allison & Busby

Nugent, Lady 2002. *Lady Nugent's Journal: Her Residence in Jamaica from 1801 to 1805* Kingston: The University of the West Indies Press

Paton, Denise 2007. Enslaved women and slavery before and after 1807: Institute of Historical Research: Newcastle: University of Newcastle

Robinson, Carey 2007. *The Iron Thorn: The defeat of the British by the Jamaican Maroons: Early Masters of Guerrilla Warfare.* Kingston: LH Publishing Limited.

Satchell, Vermont 1999. Jamaica: Http.Africana.com

Sherlock & Bennett 1998. *The Story of the Jamaican People*: Kingston: Ian Randle Publishers

Smith, K & F Smith, 1989. *To Shoot Hard Labour: The Life and Times of Sam Smith, an Antiguan workingman 1877-1982*: London: Karia Press

Stuart, Andrea 2012. *Sugar in the Blood: A Family's Story of Slavery and Empire*: London: Portobello Books

The African Caribbean Religions
Exhibition 2012 Institute of Jamaica, Kingston

Torrington, Arthur 2013. Making Freedom Conference 1838: 175 Years after Emancipation: Lectures & Exhibition: London

Tortello, Rebecca 2001. Pieces of the Past: The Road to Freedom 1834-1838: Kingston: Daily Gleaner

Tortello, Rebecca 2003. Pieces of the Past: The Magical Spiderman: Anancy Kingston: Daily Gleaner

Vansertima, Ivan 1986. They Came Before Columbus: The African Presence in Ancient America: Lecture London: Camden Town Hall